D1610998

Hollywood Costume Design

David Chierichetti

Harmony Books

For my dear parents, Anthony and Elizabeth Chierichetti

Harmony Books, a division of Crown Publishers, Inc.
419 Park Avenue South
New York, New York 10016

Published simultaneously in Canada by General Publishing Company Limited.

Printed in Great Britain

ISBN: 0-517-526379

Library of Congress Card Catalog Number: 76-6729
Chierichetti, David.
  Hollywood costume design.
1. Costume design. 2. Costume. I. Title.
TT507.054 1976 791.43'02'6 76-6729
ISBN 0-517-526379

Contents

Acknowledgement

Enormous thanks are due to Lee Plunkett whose exhaustive research into this subject got me well started and provided the majority of the credits in the film index; I also greatly appreciate the help of Milo Anderson; Lucille Ball; Joan Bennett; Stella Blum; Eddie Brandt's Saturday Matinee; Evelyn Brent; Philip Chamberlin and Mildred Simpson of the Academy of Motion Picture Arts and Sciences; Carlos Clarens; Joan L. R. Cohen, Mary H. Kahlenburg, L. Claudia Kunze, Ronald Haver and Ingrid M. Taylor of the Los Angeles County Museum of Art; Florence Cole of the Cecil B. De Mille Trust; George Cukor; Robert Cushman; Vincent Dee; Irene Dunne; George Eells; Peggy Hamilton; Vernon Harbin of RKO General; Ann Harding; Courtney Haslam of 20th Century Fox; Ronald Haver; Olivia de Havilland; Edith Head; Suzanne Hoffman; René Hubert; Grady Hunt; Dorothy Jeakins; Deborah Kerr; Dorothy Lamour; Mitchell Leisen; Charles LeMaire; Jean Louis; Myrna Loy; Earl Luick; Leonard Maltin; Frances Mercer; Hal Mohr; Stanley Musgrove; Al Nickel and Bob Niewarner of Western Costume; Sheila O'Brien; Walter Plunkett; Marion Price; Renie; Leah Rhodes; Shannon Rogers; Helen Rose; Royer; Anne Schlosser of Charles Feldman Library of the American Film Institute; Inez Schrodt; George Seaton; Vincent Sherman; Howard Shoup; Joseph Simms; Richard Simonton Jr; Edward Stevenson; Gloria Swanson; William Travilla; Lou Valintino; Natalie Visart; Diana Vreeland; Gwen Wakeling; William G. Wong; Yvonne Wood; Michael Woulfe; Loretta Young. I would also like to give special thanks to John Kobal, who helped me with a great number of the photographs in this book.

The designers credited in the captions are those responsible for the costumes appearing in the pictures; other designers may also have been involved in the film.

Foreword by Edith Head

I am extremely pleased to see that a book has been written which captures the great contribution the costume designers have made to the visual language of motion pictures. We work in collaboration with the other creators of the film art, dealing with all periods and types of characters. It is a world of glamour and excitement, but also of research and hard work and long hours.

Speaking on behalf of the Costume Designers' Guild, I am delighted that David Chierichetti has presented the whole story of the motion picture costume designers with integrity, accuracy and charm. Starting at the very beginning, he has brought back to light many talented designers of the earliest days who had been forgotten through the years. Finally, we are all, as a group, getting the recognition we deserve.

Edith Head

Introduction

Among the many people in Hollywood who manufactured films for the world, the costume designer had a key role to play. Because costume designing can call for the most subtle mixture of fact and imagination, some of Hollywood's most creative brains were deployed in that field. The range open to them was wide: if a picture called for realism, then they had to see the actors were dressed suitably for their roles; if the studio wanted a historical drama – some fiction and some history – then the designer would be required to pay some respect to the clothes people wore in the past, but, at the same time not suppress imagination altogether. Finally, of course, came pure designing: making clothes quite out of reach of the ordinary movie-goer, and creating that aura of glamour and exoticism so important to the fantasies Hollywood dreamed up.

But although it did produce some notably realistic films – and Warner Brothers was famous for its realist films – Hollwood is principally remembered for the way it ignored reality. What people actually wore, whether in the present or the past, was largely lost sight of in the efforts to instil films with mystique. This reached a pitch in the thirties with the creation of such stars as Garbo, Dietrich, Crawford, and Davis. Actresses were raw material worked on by technicians: the make-up artist and the lighting cameraman would mould the face, the costume designer moulded and decorated the body. The rise and fall (and rise) of the costume designer parallels that of the star system.

In the earliest days there were no designers: actors and actresses wore their own clothes (so ladies with good wardrobes found they got more jobs), and serviceable period costumes could be rented from many theatrical costumers serving the broadway stage, opera and ballet companies. By 1920 most production companies had moved from New York to California, and the era of the super-efficient studio which mass-produced films had begun. Actresses working an average of fourteen hours a day, six days a week, no longer had time to go to stores or dressmakers off the studio lot for their gowns; moreover, most films were conceived in a fantasy world far removed from everyday reality and this demanded a special kind of bizarre and gaudy clothes. Furthermore, expertise was needed to overcome the technical problems. The orthochromatic film that was in general use in those days distorted colours: reds and yellows photographed unnaturally dark – for *The Merry Widow* (1925) Mae Murray wore a dress that appeared to be black velvet, but in reality was carmine – and the purest blues faded to white. Costume designing became a specialized role, calling for special talents.

Labour and materials were relatively inexpensive and in order to keep up with the frantic schedules, great numbers of garments were made on very short notice. The Western Costume Company, which originally had serviced westerns, but subsequently moved into other fields, had been founded in 1912 and there were also several smaller costumiers, but in the 1920s their stock was limited and studios frequently had to make costumes for the extras as well as the stars. By the end of the decade and the coming of talking pictures, every studio had at least one designer, many sketch artists, wardrobe men and women, and seamstresses.

Talking pictures brought a flock of new problems to the designers. Since the crude microphones seemed determined to pick up every noise except the actors' voices, the most popular fabrics, including tulle, satin and tissue taffeta, had to be eliminated because they rustled too much. The consequent concentration on velvets, soft wools and crêpes pushed the designers quickly into the figure moulding lines of the thirties. Again the twenties jewellery, such as bangle bracelets, ropes of pearls and even pendant ear-rings, all jangled on the track. If jewellery was worn at all, it had to be backed with felt; more often the designers sewed the pearls and rhinestones on to the dresses.

The development of colour films brought other problems. The first Technicolor process using two colours (a salmon pink and a complimentary dull green with shades of brown in between), referred to as two-strip, was introduced in the twenties, but did not come into common use until 1929–31. The colours were unnatural, the film was exceedingly grainy and lacking in detail and required enormous amounts of light to photograph. Three-strip Technicolor, first used in live action scenes in 1934, used a dye system of dull red, blue and yellow, later changed to magenta, cyan and yellow. When complaints were raised about the too brilliant hues it produced, the Technicolor consultants, headed by Mrs Natalie Kalmus, restricted costume designers and art directors to the dullest possible colours, especially avoiding red, for several years. Films such as *The Wizard of Oz* led to a relaxation of these rules and Technicolor became very garish for a while. Once Technicolor's process proved to be even slightly practical and popular with the public, all studios wanted more colour films than the labs could turn out, which is why it took much politicking to get a Technicolor commitment. If films were switched from black and white to colour or vice versa at the last moment, designers were faced with recolouring whole wardrobes – re-dying, bleaching or replacing garments. Cinemascope, introduced in 1953, brought different problems for the designers, because the magnifications were so much greater that detail became extremely important. For example, period costumes had to be sewn by hand, because the machine stitching became too apparent.

During the thirties, screen fashions became more simple. While often extravagant, they also tried to be elegant and, above all, smart. It was the decade when the ladies of the silver screen had the greatest influence on the attire of women all around the world. The clothes were too elaborate for the average woman to copy exactly, but she picked up whatever she could. Because Garbo sported berets in private life, millions of girls started wearing them too. Jean Harlow's platinum locks started a flurry of hair bleaching while, later on, the sensational appearance of Hedy Lamarr in 1938 caused many others to dye their hair black. The first time Joan Crawford drastically enlarged the outer corners of her upper lip for *Sadie Thompson* (1932), she was widely criticized, but then almost universally copied. Even when, in 1938, the French magazine *Marie Clare* sensibly advised its readers against the Crawford mouth unless, like Crawford, they had 'hippopotamus eyes' to balance it, it did so to no avail. The vogue for padded shoulders was even more indicative of Hollywood's role; legend has it that Crawford and Adrian initiated the trend in 1932 with *Letty Lynton*, while some claim that Schiaparelli had already launched the idea in Paris; indeed, padded shoulders had already been seen in the work of other Hollywood designers a year or two earlier. Yet, the legend contains a strong measure of truth. It was only when the idea was carried by a big star in a commercial hit that it caught on.

The second world war and its austerity programmes cut into the traditional

Hollywood dazzle. One directive from Washington, known as L85, forbade designers the use of such fabric-consuming trimmings as patch pockets and cuffs on trousers, while another order set a $5000 ceiling on new materials for each film. While this was not very strictly adhered to, there were virtually no fine fabrics available. Those studios with good stores of pre-war fabrics in stock managed very well, the others limped along on sleazy rayons and cottons splashily printed to hide defects in manufacture. Period costumes were usually very much updated; regardless of when the story took place, actresses clung to their shoulder pads and if it was set in the last twenty years, producers wanted it played in modern dress so the extras could wear their own clothes and spare the studio the expense of dressing them.

Although, as the war drew to an end Edith Head and Irene predicted that skirt hems would go down when the shortages were lifted, the drastic changes of the New Look introduced by Dior in 1947 took everybody by surprise and, since most studios had a year's backlog of unrealeased films, it was not until 1948 that the New Look came to the screen.

Despite the decrease in film production caused by television in the 1950s, most film designers continued to be active because the introduction of such wide-screen processes as Cinemascope, Vistavision and Todd-AO, the increasingly frequent use of colour and the proliferation of epic tales all made production details such as costumes more important than ever. By the mid-1960s this situation had completely reversed: large-scale musicals and epics had mostly ceased production, throwing designers out of work. The concept of a highly glamorous, beautifully dressed female star was almost totally a thing of the past. With hard reality the order of the day, clothes for most modern dress pictures were simply bought in stores, film stocks and lighting equipment had been perfected to the point where the technical expertise of the designers was not as crucial as it had once been, and indeed many films now carried no designer credits at all.

Nowadays, however, designers seem to be regaining some of their former importance. The economic recession of the early 1970s greatly increased the numbers of film-goers. Individual, attractive and even sexually provocative stars are more important than ever. The popularity of such films as *Chinatown* (1974), *The Great Gatsby* (1975) and *Funny Lady* (1975) started a wave of nostalgic films, each requiring months of preparation from the designer. Moreover, television screenings of thirties and forties movies have made audiences very knowledge-able about period styles, and modern clothes can no longer be passed off as period costumes.

Many film historians cite 1950 as the end of the 'golden age of Hollywood'. While the coming of television did cause widespread changes in the film industry, some of these benefitted the designers, so it would be inappropriate to end this history in the fifties. Instead, the chronicle of each studio's design department has been carried up to the point when the last of the contract designers left, a symbolic moment for the demise of the designer's role. The new influx of talented designers who began their careers after 1950 have not been discussed, and their creations must await a future chronicle.

Finally the roll call of great designers in this book should not obscure the fact that thousands of expert seamstresses, cutters and fitters, milliners and wardrobe men and women, working long hours with little reward, made the brilliant concepts reality. The giants of Hollywood stand on their shoulders and, although they are not named here, their contribution should not pass unnoticed.

MGM Sparkle

previous page Adrian: Joan Crawford in *Susan and God* (1940).

MGM was the most glorious of all the Hollywood studios, and for over twenty-five years it stood for splendour in everything, especially costumes. The great wealth of the studio was displayed in every possible way; clothes were often extreme in style and unrealistically lavish for the characters who were wearing them. They reached their zenith in the 1930s under the masterful design of Adrian Rosenberg. However, until then, the MGM wardrobe department was like a hotel, with designers coming and going but none staying more than a couple of years.

The first company to use the Culver City studio was Triangle whose designer, Peggy Hamilton, was very probably the first to be put under contract at any studio. Arriving in the summer of 1918, Hamilton designed for Alma Reubens and had the distinction of being the first to design for Gloria Swanson. Early in 1920, Triangle sold the studio to the Goldwyn company and Peggy Hamilton left; she would later conduct the fashion page of the Los Angeles Times and did much to promote Hollywood designers.

The wardrobe of the Goldwyn lot had been under the supervision of Sophie Wachner who ran a fashionable shop on Hollywood Boulevard at the same time. After Goldwyn merged with Metro in 1923, Wachner left and Mrs Ethel Chaffin came from Paramount to design some films and supervise the other designers.

These included the brilliant Erté who was already well known in the United States for his *Harpers Bazaar* covers. He was brought to Hollywood with great fanfare in March 1925 to work on a film called *Paris* (1926) but as the script was not yet ready, he helped with three others. Somehow the final garments were never as impressive as Erté's bizarre sketches. *La Bohème* (1926) was fraught with disagreements because Erté envisaged Mimi in crisp cottons while Lillian Gish wanted ragged silks, and Renée Adoree refused to wear corsets. Erté worked on other films, but when the script for *Paris* finally arrived, it presented what he considered to be a very distorted view of Paris as he knew it and he asked to be released from his contract.

Late in 1925 Andre-Ani arrived on the Culver City lot. Many of the Ani films were shared with the team of Maude Marsh and Kathleen Kay, fashionable dressmakers who had been brought to MGM to please Mae Murray. The team of Ani, Marsh and Kay was further enlarged on the first two Garbo films *The Temptress* and *The Torrent* (both 1926) by Max Ree, a well known theatrical designer. It is impossible now to ascertain who did what on these films, although Ree is due credit for Garbo's mammoth neck-concealing fur coat in *The Torrent*. Unfortunately all these designers left within eighteen months and MGM had to find replacements.

They used René Hubert several times between 1927 and 1933. He designed Marion Davies' lavish *Quality Street* (1927) and also worked on the first two attempts to make Tolstoy's *Anna Karenina* into a film starring Greta Garbo. When it was eventually filmed, Hubert was no longer available and the additional costumes needed were designed by Gilbert Clark.

Clark had been one of Lady Duff Gordon's designers in London and later ran a fashionable shop in New York. He was, in the words of Howard Greer, 'more

Andre-Ani: Norma Shearer in *Upstage* (1926); an outfit that shows the influence of Art Deco.

temperamental than the stars he was called upon to dress', and after Garbo complained bitterly about working with him on *The Mysterious Lady* (1928) his option was not picked up. However, David Cox, who had been Clark's assistant, stayed on until 1931 and became a fully-fledged designer. He did Joan Crawford's famous beaded charleston dress for *Our Dancing Daughters* (1928) and the rest of her films until the arrival of Adrian.

Adrian Rosenberg's career started in Paris studying design at Parson's. He went to New York at the invitation of Irving Berlin, and then to Hollywood when Natacha Rambova offered him the job of designing *What Price Beauty* (1924). The plot of the film includes a dream sequence in which the heroine wanders through a highly modernistic beauty parlour and sees models on pedestals, all wearing clothes illustrating different 'looks'. Myrna Loy, as the 'intellectual' type wears tailored red velvet pyjamas and a wig that comes to little points on her forehead. Subsequently Adrian designed for two Valentino films.

Mitchell Leisen, art director for the independent company that Cecil B. De Mille was then forming, offered Adrian a contract. He worked there for about two years, and among other things, designed two De Mille epics, *The Road to Yesterday* (1925) and *The Volga Boatman* (1926). Bouffant skirts were the new fashion at the time *Volga Boatman* was being filmed, but De Mille wanted tight dresses which moulded the women's hips. So Adrian created gowns that were tight to the thighs and then exploded into extravagant fullness. Although they received no credit, both Adrian and Mitchell Leisen contributed some costumes to De Mille's greatest epic, *The King of Kings* (1927), which was officially designed by Gwen Wakeling and Earl Luick.

De Mille and his company moved to MGM in the summer of 1928. Since their first film *Dynamite* was not to begin shooting for six months, Adrian was assigned to other MGM productions, including several with Garbo.

Dynamite (1929) proved to be a rather ordinary assignment, but the next De Mille epic, *Madame Satan* (1930) contained a party sequence on a Zeppelin that was one of the wildest things Adrian ever designed. As the guests enter the party, each recites a verse explaining his costume. A young woman covered by a few carefully placed fans announces that she is 'Miss Movie Fan' while another appears in an enormous afro wig made of lambswool and says, 'Have no fear my child, I'm the call of the wild'. Henry VIII appears with six wives, all dressed in sparkling cellophane. Finally Kay Johnson enters in a black velvet cloak, the back covered with an enormous serpent head rendered in half-inch white and mother-of-pearl sequins. 'Which one of you is man enough to go to hell with Madame Satan?' she asks.

The *Madame Satan* party and a fashion show in the Joan Crawford vehicle *Our Blushing Brides* (both 1930) featured what would be the major traits of Adrian's designing for the rest of his film career. He tried to avoid middle greys as much as possible and contrasted blacks and whites, knowing that these would create the greatest impact within the confines of monochrome film. It was in line with MGM's constant use of white in the sets and their emphasis on production values, often to the detriment of the dramatic values of a film. Traditionally pure blacks and whites were avoided because they were difficult to photograph: white clad figures went out of focus and had haloes, and black registered like the inside of a hole with no detail whatsoever. Navy blues and beiges that looked black and white on the screen were often substituted, but Adrian insisted that the real shades would carry more impact and MGM had the time and money to learn how to photograph them. As early as 1931, Peggy Hamilton gave a showing of costumes from Adrian's films and every single one was black and white. Even

Adrian: some of the costumes worn at the party in *Madam Satan* (1930).

Adrian's working sketches were rendered in the same blacks, whites and greys they would appear in the film, instead of the pretty colours designers usually used. Sometimes the clothes would then be made in bright colours from the monochromatic sketch so the actresses would not get too depressed wearing them.

Adrian had a passion for straight lines. Not only did he square shoulders with padding, he often draped the waistlines of his frocks loosely to fill in the indentation. He created the most severely tailored suits anybody had ever seen. He loved glitter and used sequins and brilliants with abandon. His use of glitter on white organdie or tulle ruffles was so well known within the industry it was almost a joke. He used bows constantly: big ones that stretched across Ann Harding from shoulder to shoulder in *Biography of a Bachelor Girl* (1935), scores of black ones on Jean Harlow's white sleeves in *Hold Your Man* (1932), almost imperceptible bows stuck on handbags and the back of hats. 'Whenever Adrian has a problem with some part of a costume, he sticks a bow over it', sighed Luise Rainer.

Adrian was highly productive and even on mammoth productions like *Marie Antoinette* (1938) and *The Wizard of Oz* (1939) he designed everything, including the extras' clothes, throwing out sketches every two or three minutes. His work with his superstars was far more exacting, and he dealt with each in a different way. If some of these clothes now appear excessively theatrical, it must be remembered they were appropriate to MGM's kind of movies and the stars MGM created.

The most extreme Adrian designs were usually intended for Joan Crawford. Her whole appearance was an overstatement: enormous eyes, enlarged mouth. This heady movie star presence overwhelmed conventional clothes and they did not look good on her figure with its broad shoulders, long waist and short legs. Trying to find a new device to make Crawford's hips seem narrower, Adrian hit

Adrian: Joan Crawford in *Letty Lynton* (1932); the dress that began the swing towards padded shoulders.

upon the idea of making her shoulders even broader by enveloping them in voluminous ruffles for *Letty Lynton* (1932). By comparison her hips seemed smaller and the costume put them both on the fashion map. Although the dress was seen only briefly, it caused such a sensation that thousands of copies were made for the retail market. Adrian later remarked, 'Who would ever believe that my whole career would rest on Joan Crawford's shoulders!' After the ruffles came shoulder pads, which not only broadened Crawford's shoulders but also squared them off. They first appeared in a tailored dress in *Today We Live* (1933) and then in most of Crawford's outfits after that.

Adrian thought that the frequent use of close-ups in a film, especially when the face was as extraordinary as that of Crawford or Garbo, made it a good idea to keep the important details of a costume above the waist. For *Forsaking all*

opposite
Adrian's adventures in black and white

top left Joan Crawford in *No More Ladies* (1935),
bottom left Ann Harding in *Biography of a Bachelor Girl* (1934),
top right Luise Rainer in *The Toy Wife* (1938),
bottom right Joan Crawford in *Dancing Lady* (1933).

Others (1934) he made Crawford a dark coat with a white plate collar that extended beyond her shoulders and rose up behind her head. *No More Ladies* (1935) found her wearing an enormous starched white collar that looked like two sails and extended so far over her arms that she was unable to get a cigarette up to her mouth.

Adrian, who dressed her between 1929 and 1941, enjoyed working with Greta Garbo since she had his ideal figure: square shouldered, with only the very slightest indentation at the waist and straight hips, there were no curves anywhere for him to straighten out. This was fine for Garbo's highly stylized modern dress films but for the period films for which she is now best remembered, it took all of Adrian's expertise to soften her stark contours. Like Crawford, Garbo had broad shoulders, but Adrian worked to de-emphasize them. In her modern dress pictures, he cheated her shoulder seams up and enveloped them in kimono sleeves and other drapery. For Garbo, Adrian created the heroines of history and

Adrian: Joan Crawford in *No More Ladies* (1935); the collar was so big that Crawford could not lift her cigarette to her mouth.

opposite
Adrian and Greta Garbo on the set of *The Single Standard* (1929).

literature with his clothes. She depended on them for her performance. Arriving early in the morning, she would put on her costume and staring into a mirror would rehearse the day's scenes until she was satisfied that they were perfect, seeing how she could use the sleeves and skirts for her dramatic purpose.

Romance (1930) supposedly took place in the 1850s, though Adrian stylized the concept so much it looked little like any period of the nineteenth century. He placed a flat Eugénie hat, complete with an enormous black plume, on Garbo's head and positioned it at a very steep angle. To a generation of women tired of cloches and helmets, the Eugénie was the answer. With or without the plume, that angle over one eye dominated women's hats for the rest of the decade. *Mata Hari* (1932) was an enjoyable exercise in elaborate beading on velvet, gold mesh clothes and skullcaps, but the severe, historically accurate costumes of *Queen Christina* (1933) were more beautiful. The most famous was a stark black velvet with a plate collar that encircled Garbo's head. It had sleeves that were tight to

Adrian: Greta Garbo in *The Kiss* (1929); the dress shows what her figure was like.

just above the elbow where they burst into fullness, the only ornamentation on the costume and a device which filled in her waistline without adding to her shoulders. *Anna Karenina* (1935) was an elaborate period work without any stylization. For the croquet scene, Adrian surrounded Garbo for the first time in the masses of white ruffles he had often used on Crawford and Shearer. No longer dramatic and mysterious, she became momentarily light hearted and romantic.

Camille (1936) was one of Adrian's best efforts to interpret the story through
the clothes. While the standard Adrian blacks and whites are used to indicate the
blatant promiscuity of Olympe, played by Lenore Ulric, Garbo's clothes in the
first sequences are purposefully understated. In the first scene in the theatre, her
costume is a modestly embroidered silk coat trimmed in red fox while Lenore
Ulric wears a fluffy white dress trimmed with enormous black sequins. At the
auction Ulric wears one of the starkest black and white faille ensembles Adrian
ever made, while Garbo's costume is a soft lead grey velvet, profusely but subtly
embroidered at the shoulders and cuffs with steel grey beads. The contrast
between Marguerite Gautier's profession as courtesan and her essential purity of
spirit is epitomized by the gown Garbo wears in the party sequence. Adrian gave
her his usual trademarks, a white chiffon dress sprinkled with silver stars and a
big black bow at the neckline, but while the other women are decked out in
elaborate necklaces of paste diamonds* Garbo wears heavy gold chains at her
neck and wrists, a device intended to emphasize her strength and refinement.

Another star to benefit greatly from Adrian's expertise was Jeanette
MacDonald who looked more attractive in her MGM films than she had before.
For *Merry Widow* (1934), Adrian's staff created foundation garments that re-
shaped her figure magnificently and while Adrian kept the lines of the 1880s for

* MGM sometimes sent Adrian to Europe to do research and once he came back with a
museum quality collection of paste jewellery which was copied and used in both *Camille* and
Conquest (1937).

Adrian: Jeanette MacDonald in *Merry Widow* (1934).

her dresses, he executed them in the wispiest of chiffons and voiles which trans- mitted light and moved beautifully. Ali Hubert who designed for the rest of the cast followed suit, and the dancers' gowns floated effortlessly despite their bulk.

As she grew thinner, MacDonald's face and neck began to look very long, so Adrian designed hats that were high off her face and extremely wide. Her wigs now had curls at the side to add width to her face, and as often as possible Adrian covered up her neck with high collars or complicated chokers. These problems aside, her figure became a dream to dress. With long legs and no hips, she could wear pencil-thin Empire gowns that Adrian could not put on any other stars.

Sweethearts (1938) gave Adrian his first real chance to work in the medium of 3-strip Technicolor. Adrian created as much visual excitement in colour as he had in black and white; but here there were no sharp contrasts, only softly harmonizing colours. The usual difficulties in dealing with Technicolor were magnified in this case because it had been designed as a black and white film and was only Technicolored at the last minute when MGM postponed *Northwest*

Passage. Rather than copy her natural light brown hair, the studio decided to make Jeanette MacDonald's wigs a bright red that harmonized well with her sea green eyes. Exhaustive tests were made until the right shade of orange hair was found and then the hair and the eyes became the central colours around which MacDonald's whole wardrobe was designed. Disregarding the then-popular notion that redheads shouldn't wear pink, Adrian kept her in a certain pale pink shade through much of the picture. It was a metaphor for the character she played: a spoiled, bored heroine of a saccharine operetta. The play within the film was a harmless parody of earlier MacDonald-Eddy films, and the silly pink tulle and gold sequined dress was a parody of all the tulle and sequined dresses Adrian had made for MacDonald and the others over the years.

Adrian also dressed Norma Shearer whose husband Irving Thalberg cast her as a wealthy adulterous wife in shockers like *Riptide* (1934), which opened with a very glittering ball to which all the guests came dressed as bugs. Adrian designed her siren clothes with deep décolletages and very tight bias draping of her hips and thighs, which, if she stood just so, could be highly provocative. Adrian made the biggest fashion news with Shearer when he put her in a light suit with a dark blouse in *The Divorcee* (1930).

Lest the public get tired of Shearer as a seductress, Thalberg interspersed some romantic heroine roles for her such as the lead in *Romeo and Juliet* (1936). The celebrated stage designer, Oliver Messel, came from London especially for this film. Arriving at MGM, he found that Thalberg had also assigned Adrian to it, but in the end Messel did all the sets, all the men's and more than half of the women's costumes, including some for Shearer.

Adrian designed *Marie Antoinette* (1938), Shearer's next film. While his costumes acknowledged the essential shapes of the era, they were otherwise a flight of exquisite fantasy. So great was the cost of costumes and sets that the studio had to compensate by finding a faster director. The final film was opulent beyond compare but sadly unconvincing dramatically.

Adrian made Shearer's phony countess in *Idiot's Delight* (1939) a creature of amusingly slinky draperies, but Shearer was noticeably plumper in *The Women* (1939) so he raised her waistline and made her skirts fuller. Reflecting the great interest in *Gone With the Wind*, Shearer wore an 1860s influenced ballgown, the enormous crinoline harmonizing with her chubby arms. For the climax of the film, Adrian made Shearer in gold lamé confront Joan Crawford in gold sequins; Shearer got her man back, but Crawford's glitter out-dazzled her.

The lovable vulgarity of Jean Harlow's usual screen character inspired Adrian's funniest clothes. In *Red Dust* (1932) he gave her kimonos that had no sashes or other fastenings and depended on Jean's arms to keep closed. When she made exclamatory gestures, the robe would start to separate alarmingly, but Harlow always managed to get it back together before it was too late.

Other glamorous stars at MGM, even though their stays were brief, got the full Adrian treatment. At the time of her one MGM film, *Faithless* (1932) Adrian said, 'Tallulah Bankhead can wear more silver fox than almost any other woman and still look under-dressed'. Constance Bennett, painfully thin, still got her backless evening gowns, but they concealed her protruding shoulder blades and smoothed her jagged hipbones.

Myrna Loy was the only major star at MGM that Adrian did not always dress satisfactorily. Unlike Crawford and Garbo whose overwhelming presences needed incredible clothes, Loy's acting was powerful in its underplaying. If she wore clothes with too many clever details, they distracted from the subtlety of her performance. For instance, Adrian once trimmed the front of her dress with his

Adrian: Jean Harlow in *Reckless* (1935).

Adrian: A seductive Norma Shearer in
Riptide (1934).

opposite
Adrian: the confrontation between
Gladys George and Norma Shearer in
Marie Antoinette (1938).

favourite big, round buttons, but after the film's preview, Loy's husband remarked, 'Those buttons completely erased your face, Myrna.' Adrian's designs for Loy's one period film, *Parnell* (1938) were exquisite, but the quiet sophistication of her other films was more suited to Dolly Tree, MGM's second-string designer.

Dolly Tree was a bright young woman from England who had worked for Fox before coming to MGM in 1934. At first she got assignments for films that lacked a big female star, but later she designed three films for Harlow in her dark blonde period and then two for Judy Garland.

Despite all the attention MGM gave its female stars, the men handled their screen wardrobes in modern dress films themselves (sometimes in consultation with their directors) and were reimbursed by the studio. Period men, military uniforms and ethnic costumes were designed by Lucia 'Mother' Coulter, who came to MGM from Universal in 1925. After her death in 1936, Gile Steel began designing for men in period films like *Marie Antoinette* (1938).

As the decade drew to a close, the era of glamour at MGM represented by Adrian's clothes was ending too. Of the new stars, only Hedy Lamarr and Greer Garson were suited to elegant, formal clothes. Garbo, Crawford, Shearer, MacDonald and Loy had all left MGM by 1942.

Late in Adrian's tenure at MGM came *The Wizard of Oz* (1939) which utilized his flair for the fantastic more than any other film. He persuaded Technicolor's Natalie Kalmus to use more bright colours together than Technicolor had permitted since *Becky Sharp* (1935). When it had proved impossible to borrow

opposite
Adrian: Myrna Loy and Clark Gable in *Parnell* (1938).

Dolly Tree visits Myrna Loy on the set of *Manhattan Melodrama* (1934).

Shirley Temple from Fox to play Dorothy, Adrian was asked to make Judy Garland appear younger instead. His first idea, complete with blonde wig, was not a success, so a second dress, illustrated here, was designed. Garland's naturally high waistline was raised even higher, a long hairpiece covered her breasts, and elbow length sleeves obscured the contours of the sides of her figure. Evidently this was not convincing either, and when MGM finally decided to play Dorothy as an adolescent, the now familiar blue gingham dress was designed. It had a definite waistline over a tight corset, short sleeves and more refined trimmings.

Adrian designed once again for Garland as well as Hedy Lamarr and Lana Turner in the Busby Berkeley spectacular, *Ziegfeld Girl* (1941). The 'You stepped Out of a Dream' number was typical high white MGM decor with Turner and Lamarr glistening in yet more editions of the chiffon, tulle and silver stars special, and Garland covered by a shapeless shimmer of silver foil. The 'Minnie from Trinidad' number was far more inventive. Garland's dress pushed her waistline down almost nine inches, while Lamarr carried mammoth orchids on her bust, right hip and head, as more orchids sprouted from tree trunks in a rain forest.

opposite
Adrian: Judy Garland in a test for a costume that was not used in *The Wizard of Oz* (1939).

Adrian: Hedy Lamarr, Judy Garland and Lana Turner in the 'Minnie from Trinidad' number from *Ziegfeld Girl* (1940).

However, various problems were making Adrian increasingly unsettled at MGM. Having gone through the Depression spending freely, the studio began imposing budgets on him, telling him to use rayons instead of silks just as film revenues began going up. Gradually he began to lose his autonomy. Sometimes he had to make several sketches before he did one that pleased everybody. George Cukor rejected the whole wardrobe for *Two Faced Woman* (1941) and told Adrian to make simple garments like those Garbo wore in her private life. Adrian apparently complied since he gets credit for the film, but he knew his era was over and when his contract expired in 1941, he opened his own couture shop and did two highly profitable collections a year. Clothes from his shop appeared on actresses in many films, but he did not again design a picture in the true sense. MGM sought him out for *Lovely to Look At* (1951) but Adrian made everything in his own workroom and kept his involvement with MGM minimal.

About the time of Adrian's departure there were several changes of designers at MGM. Dolly Tree left, and Howard Shoup was brought in from Warners and Robert Kalloch from Columbia, but neither stayed very long. Robert Kalloch's designs were similar to Adrian's and he did three films with Lana Turner, two with Greer Garson and one with Norma Shearer. Shoup stayed on to work under Irene's supervision, and did several films before being drafted into the Air Force.

After Adrian had left, Irene Lentz Gibbons came to MGM as supervising designer. She had been a movie extra and piano student who began by making clothes for her friends and eventually became the leading couturiere on the west coast. Stars bought their personal wardrobes from her and began to use her for their films as well.

Nobody could match Irene's virtuosity when it came to souffle. Her soft crepes and chiffons were meant to be worn without brassieres, but there was a discreet construction underneath which lifted the breasts delicately, augmented them if they were meagre and allowed the nipples to show through. She also padded hips when need be. Irene's fit was so exact that the slightest change in weight caused problems. She was equally renowned for her suits which were tailored, full of choice detail, yet softly feminine.

The interests of glamour for its own sake in the best tradition of MGM were well served by Irene. Dramatically, *Weekend at the Waldorf* (1945) was the epitome of cold insincerity, but as a vehicle for Irene's marvellous clothes, it was sublime. A spiral of jewels was placed at one side of Ginger Rogers' towering pompadour, from the middle came a spray of coq feathers and the finest of veils was draped around her whole head. Cuffs jewelled in the same pattern came down the back of her hands to her fingers and she carried sables.

Versatile Irene was not. She could relate to actresses like Stanwyck, Loretta Young, Katharine Hepburn and Joan Crawford because they were women much like Irene herself: intelligent, sophisticated and with perfect posture. She was not interested in MGM's ingénue types like June Allyson and Gloria de Haven and they were dressed by members of her staff which included Kay Dean and Marion Herwood Keyes, while Valles did all the men's costumes.

Irene's department was weak in period and musical design, and more help had to be brought in. When the *Gaslight* (1943) wardrobe first went into work, it had not been designed at all but rather copied exactly from old engravings. George Cukor was not satisfied and so Irene brought in Madame Barbara Karinska, who had built costumes for ballets and musicals all over Europe. She designed and executed the most intricate bustles and flounces MGM had ever seen then, stayed on to do the fantastic *Kismet* (1944). Both times Irene was listed as the designer, but studio employees now say that she really had no part in them at all.

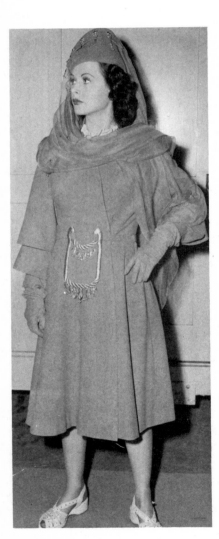

Marion Herwood Keyes: Hedy Lamarr in a costume test for *Her Highness and the Bellboy* (1945); Lamarr's pregnancy was concealed with full sleeves and many draped veils.

Irene: a sketch for a suit for Barbara
Stanwyck in *B.F.'s Daughter* (1948).

33

Irene fits a dress on Lana Turner for *Slightly Dangerous* (1943).

opposite
Madame Karinska: Ingrid Bergman in one of her dresses for *Gaslight* (1943), showing the marked Italian flavour.

Irene Sharaff was also brought in from Broadway to help with MGM's musicals. After designing for Eleanor Powell and Lena Horne in *I Dood It* (1943), then for Garland and Rooney in *Girl Crazy* (1943), Sharaff was given a very different assignment: sombre Parisian clothes of the 1890s for *Madame Curie* (1943). Sharaff had a superb sense of colour which is evident in the Christmas Eve ball in *Meet Me in St Louis* (1944), her first collaboration with Vincente Minnelli. At first there was opposition from the Technicolor consultant to the idea of putting Judy Garland in a deep red velvet dress next to Lucille Bremer in emerald green in a red plush room, full of extras in fluffy pastels. Despite their misgivings, it worked well visually, and it was highly effective dramatically. It made Garland more passionate than the ingénues she had been playing, and added impact to the following scene in which she sings 'Have Yourself a Merry Little Christmas'.

More help was needed for musicals and period films. Studio head Louis B. Mayer preferred the garish look of the Fox musicals to Sharaff's tasteful and accurate period work and without consulting Irene, he hired Helen Rose, a Fox designer, for musicals in 1943, but it was over a year before Irene allowed her to

work on *Ziegfeld Follies* (1946) with Sharaff. Then in 1945 Walter Plunkett arrived to specialize in period and ethnic costumes. Plunkett's first assignments were small, but then came the epic *Green Dolphin Street* (1947) which required months of preparation to furnish the many changes needed by Lana Turner, Donna Reed and Gladys Cooper. The 1830s with their big sleeves, flared but not very full skirts and laced slippers, was an unusual period for films and there was very little in stock for either the extras or the stars. Plunkett also had to do a lot of research into the dress of the nineteenth century Maoris.

At the same time Plunkett had two assignments with Katharine Hepburn, his favourite actress. *Sea of Grass* (1947) cast her as a wealthy pioneer woman of the 1880s, while in *Song of Love* (1947) she protrayed Klara Schumann. In 1949 he worked for Hepburn again when he made a rare and highly successful excursion into contemporary fashions doing *Adam's Rib* (1949).

Plunkett also designed costumes for *Summer Holiday* (1948), but the colour scheme was the idea of the director, Rouben Mamoulian. Mamoulian decided to return to the colours people actually wore during the hot summers of the turn of the century: whites, pale blues and greys, and leave the strong colours to the trees, skies and red bricks of the houses. Bright colour was saved for a scene when Mickey Rooney meets Marilyn Maxwell and gets drunk. The first dress is sickly pink with a little hat carrying one scrawny black feather. As Rooney gets

Irene Sharaff: Mary Astor in *Meet Me in St Louis* (1944); an example of the kind of very accurate period work which Arthur Freed and Vincente Minnelli liked, but which L. B. Mayer did not.

Irene Sharaff: Greer Garson in *Madame Curie* (1943).

opposite
Madame Karinska: Marlene Dietrich in a costume test for *Kismet* (1944).

drunker, Maxwell begins to look more beautiful to him. The dress becomes a deeper, prettier pink. This continues through four dresses until Rooney is completely inebriated and Maxwell's dress is deep red, the enormous red hat covered with magnificent plumes.

Plunkett would be the last MGM designer to work with Judy Garland, MGM's top female star of the forties who was also the most difficult to dress. Howard Shoup designed for Garland when her figure was at its best: fairly slender with a pleasing fullness to her face and arms. Shoup says, 'I had her waist cinched in so tight she could hardly breathe but she wanted me to do it.' But by 1944 Garland was too thin in *Meet Me in St Louis* and Sharaff had to gather fabric to fill her out. Then her weight began to fluctuate drastically. In the short period between the filming of the two numbers that constituted her brief appearance in *Words and Music* (1948) she gained about ten pounds. Helen Rose anticipated this and designed a straight dress that would conceal a gain or loss fairly well, although sharp eyes will notice that Garland no longer has her belt on as she slips from the first song into the second.

Walter Plunkett designed and made all the costumes for *Annie Get Your Gun* (1950) at Garland's request, but when Betty Hutton took over the title role, she asked Helen Rose to do her clothes, though Plunkett's designs for the rest of the cast were retained. Plunkett also did Garland's last feature for MGM, *Summer Stock* (1950). He remembers, 'Judy liked me, and I liked her so very much. Her figure was bad then, she was too heavy, she had no waistline, and her hips started under the bustline. I was no genius at modern clothes. She was in a horrible turmoil and when it was finally over, they knew they needed to do

Walter Plunkett: two costumes tests of Judy Garland in the version of *Annie Get your Gun* (1949) which was never completed.

something, so after several weeks, she came back with a lovely figure and she did that "Get Happy" number.'

Meanwhile Irene's position at the studio was becoming precarious. Despite her great success, she was unhappy and drank heavily. Louis B. Mayer did give Irene a new contract in July 1947, but let her resume her retail business on the side, and the other designers gradually had to assume her responsibilities. This meant that Helen Rose could broaden her field of experience. As she says, 'At first I did only musicals, most of which required period costumes. The job suited me perfectly because I wasn't interested in modern clothes. Irene preferred the Irene Dunnes or the Katharine Hepburns to youngsters like Elizabeth Taylor or Jane Powell, so frequently I was asked to design their pictures.' Rose then began designing modern clothes for established stars like Lana Turner and Barbara Stanwyck too, so when the belt-tightening began around 1950, it was obvious that there was no justification for keeping Irene. As part of the cutback measures Valles was allowed to go and Plunkett began designing the mens' costumes as well as the women's on his films. He often did the men on Rose's films too, although sometimes annonymously since he did not want to get typed as a men's designer. Herschel McCoy also shared some films with Rose, and being an expert on things ancient, did *Quo Vadis* (1951), *Julius Caesar* (1953) and *The Prodigal* (1955) on his own.

Helen Rose

Herschel McCoy: Deborah Kerr and Robert Taylor on the set of *Quo Vadis* (1951).

In the fifties MGM continued to place much emphasis on glamour for its own sake while other studios, especially Paramount, were getting more involved in realism. The lines were highly romantic: the padded shoulders and girdled buttocks were replaced by small waists, long full skirts and stoles. MGM had a virtual monopoly on Hollywood's beautiful women: Elizabeth Taylor, Grace Kelly, Lana Turner, Deborah Kerr, Cyd Charisse – and Helen Rose glamourized them all. Yards of chiffon and white fox became her trademark, possibly because Lana Turner wore these in the 'mad' scene of *The Bad and the Beautiful* (1952) for which Rose won the black and white Oscar that year. The central theme of *Designing Woman* (1956) – that of a fashion designer married to a sportswriter – was Helen Rose's idea and it gave her a chance to create a luxurious wardrobe for the long, lean Lauren Bacall. Rose also designed Grace Kelly's MGM films. Of those days, she recalls, 'I loved the period, Grace was beautiful and in love with the prince and life was divine. I have always been extremely proud that Grace

Helen Rose: Deborah Kerr in *Dream Wife* (1953); a very atypical Rose creation, stark and stylized in contrast to the usual highly feminine and classically elegant lines she is famous for.

Helen Rose: Elizabeth Taylor and Paul
Newman in *Cat on a Hot Tin Roof* (1959);
the famous white chiffon V neck dress.

chose me to design her wedding gown as practically every designer in the world
vied for this honour.' *The Swan* (1956) is a rare example of MGM allowing Rose to
design a true period film. Usually they tried to avoid anything that was too
realistic. For instance, there is virtually nothing of the twenties in *Good News*
(1947), or *Words and Music* (1948). 'They always wanted it stylized', regrets
Rose today.

Elizabeth Taylor literally grew up in Helen Rose creations from the teenager
in *A Date With Judy* (1948) through the fresh beauty in love for the first time in
Father of the Bride (1950), to the voluptuous star of *Rhapsody* (1954). Rose frequently put her in a pure, brilliant colour and says, 'I had to keep her designs
very simple so they wouldn't detract from her face.' Richard Brooks wanted all
the sets and costumes of *Cat on a Hot Tin Roof* (1959) to be colourless and Taylor
to have only two changes of costume, a slip and a completely plain blouse and
skirt. But when Taylor persuaded Brooks to allow a third in the last part of the
film, Rose designed a beautiful white chiffon gown with a plunging v neckline
showing ample cleavage. Taylor asked Rose to make extra copies and variations
for her personal use, and in the following months the fan magazines were filled

with news of Taylor's romance with Eddie Fisher and pictures of her in Helen Rose's chiffon dress. Rose received so many requests for the dress that she decided to go into the wholesale garment business where she met with great success. After her contract expired in 1960 she continued to work in her own business but still found time to do occasional films.

Although other designers, such as Mary Ann Nyberg, Elizabeth Haffenden and Morton Haack, worked at MGM in the 1950s, it was Walter Plunkett who continued to draw most of the big costume assignments. He did the classic musical *Singing in the Rain* (1952). Although the period of the film was less than twenty-five years ago (usually too short a time lag for accurate costuming) Plunkett was encouraged to use the exaggerated modes of the late twenties that were Hollywood's alone. Plunkett's hats were true helmets and cloches, covering the foreheads and ears. When Debbie Reynolds did 'Good Morning', her blue-grey knit had a bolt of yellow lightning up the front, so true of the early radio-crazed days when electrical symbols abounded. Plunkett recalls, 'I didn't have to get any stills, it was all in my memory from when I started at RKO. The plus-fours Gene Kelly and Donald O'Connor wore were like outfits I had had made up for myself at the time. For the chorus girls, I got myself in the same mental attitude I had for the girls in *Flying Down to Rio*. Total absurdity. Arthur Freed and Stanley Donen began to have such a good time with it that they decided to

Walter Plunkett: Donald O'Connor, Debbie Reynolds and Gene Kelly in *Singin' in the Rain* (1952).

put in a fashion show. I would design something outrageous and they would write the verse to sing about it. ''Black is best when you're in court, the judge will be impressed, but white is right when you're a bride and want to look your best.'' Fashion shows always had to end with a bride.'

Plunkett was also assigned by Vincente Minnelli to many of his films. Their collaboration began in 1949 with *Madame Bovary*. 'Minnelli is the most demanding perfectionist but I get along with him very well. He wants perfection, but when you give it to him, he gets it up there on the screen and you're proud to be associated with him. If there's something exquisite around the hem of the skirt, tell him and he'll have her sit some way so that it shows.' Minnelli made Emma Bovary's gowns a symbol of her folly by having Jennifer Jones struggle to get her enormous skirts through the cramped little rooms she lived in.

There were three designers on Minnelli's *An American in Paris* (1951). Orry Kelly did several numbers and all the women; Walter Plunkett did the black and white ball and all the men, and Irene Sharaff did a brief series of four costumes in the multiple image sequence which introduced Leslie Caron and then all of the 'American in Paris' ballet (see page 126). Lasting twenty minutes and containing over five hundred costumes, the ballet consisted of a series of tableaux, each in the style of a different painter – Dufy, Toulouse-Lautrec, Rousseau, Renoir. The designers received the Academy Award for Best Colour Costume Design of 1951.

Irene Sharaff: a scene from the *American in Paris* (1953) ballet sequence with Leslie Caron and Gene Kelly.

Minnelli used Plunkett on several more films in the 1950s including *Some Came Running* (1958) with Shirley MacLaine. On Minnelli's instructions to 'dress her as a poor, simple, misguided little girl', Plunkett bought a stuffed dog from a toy shop and made it into a purse and made one of her dresses from a silk print of kittens. Minnelli's *Bells are Ringing* (1960) required a dress for Judy Holliday which could catch fire without burning her. 'She was utterly terrified but she needn't have been. We put several layers of asbestos between her and the fire.'

Plunkett's contract expired but he stayed on for over a year working on *How the West Was Won* (1963). He later returned for John Ford's *Seven Women* (1966) after which he retired.

The fortunes of MGM declined through the 1960s and in the spring of 1969 there was an enormous auction of props and costumes. The few remaining Adrians brought high prices and collectors were quick to snatch up the more recent creations of Rose and Plunkett. Subsequently Soundstage 25 was transformed into an enormous store in which the whole stock wardrobe was sold off at bargain prices. For the next several years, MGM's costumes of all periods became the everyday wear of students throughout Southern California.

Paramount Polish

previous page
Travis Banton: Marlene Dietrich on
The Devil is a Woman (1935); the 45°
angle is repeated and the profuse use of
lace adds bulk.

Paramount was the most important film company between 1915 and 1925. It had studios in Hollywood and New York and turned out a hundred features a year with an assembly line efficiency that made costume designers a necessity several years before ther studios thought of employing any. While tasteful, fashionable clothes had frequently been seen in films, it was Paramount's Cecil B. De Mille who first realized the commercial value of highly exaggerated modes. 'I want clothes that will make people gasp when they see them', he told the wardrobe department, 'don't design anything anybody could possibly buy in a store.'

The first of the Paramount designers was a pretty young woman named Claire West. She had worked with D. W. Griffith and was already well established at Paramount by the summer of 1918 when Mitchell Leisen arrived to work on the Babylonian costumes for De Mille's *Male and Female* (1919). West supervised all the Hollywood studio's productions for the next several years, although other designers were brought in for specific films. For example, although they received no credit, Leisen and Natacha Rambova (Rudolph Valentino's wife) worked on the dream sequence for De Mille's *Fool's Paradise* (1921).

l to r: Edith Head (Paramount), Edward Stevenson (RKO), Howard Greer (freelance) and Adrian (MGM) picnic in the country in the late 1930s.

Paramount's studios at Astoria New York had no contract designer; the costumes were handled by the actresses themselves, New York couturiers and Broadway talent. Norman Norell did three films there including Gloria Swanson's *Zaza* (1923). Of those days Swanson says 'I was never a doll for anybody to dress

up. I told them the kind of thing I wanted for each picture and they got somebody to do it.' Swanson went to France in 1925 to make *Madame Sans Gêne*. It
was designed by René Hubert. Swanson was so pleased with his costumes that
she brought him back to Hollywood with her.

Howard Greer, a New York couturier and the creator of the costumes for the
Greenwich Village Follies, was asked out to Hollywood in January, 1923. He
worked with Claire West on De Mille's *The Ten Commandments* (1923) and when
she left shortly afterwards, Greer became Paramount's chief designer. Like his
creations, Greer was theatrical and flamboyant and because the clothes had to be
designed so much in advance of the actual release of the picture, Greer once told
a reporter, 'The clothes we design up here are one year ahead of Paris and two
years ahead of the manufacturers'. The reporter retorted that some of Greer's
strange clothes 'are so far ahead of Paris that Paris never catches up with them!'
In 1926 Greer tried unsuccessfully to launch a revival of the high-waisted Empire
lines, by using them on Betty Compson in *Locked Doors* and Pola Negri in *Good
and Naughty* but the female public kept their low waists.

One of Greer's greatest assets was his ability to understand the vibrant person-
alities of the Paramount ladies and translate them into clothes. He explained,
'When I first came to Hollywood, I was frightened to death of Pola Negri. There
was a lot of publicity about what she did to people she didn't like. Pola frightens
more people than any other woman on the screen, yet to me, now, she is the
least terrifying. You simply have to understand her. Pola is really happy only
when she is wearing rags, and she is more particular about the rags than the
elaborate gowns. But if Pola's raiment is to be gorgeous, it must be super-so.
Betty Compson is adorable in the "gamin" sort of clothes, something in which
she can look the least bit tough, although she can wear anything. Lois Wilson,
poor girl, seems doomed never to get out of the Sears Roebuck class. We open

René Hubert and Gloria Swanson discuss
the fashions for *The Coast of Folly* (1926).

catalogues to get the sort of thing the Middle West is wearing. They must be attractive but not too smart. Perhaps we'd do better if we bought them.'

Paramount acquired a second top designer late in 1924 when Travis Banton was brought in for a high fashion picture, *The Dressmaker from Paris* (1925). He had been a designer with the famous Madame Frances in New York and had also achieved some celebrity when Mary Pickford chose a wedding gown that he had designed for her secret marriage to Douglas Fairbanks. Greer and Banton divided the Paramount assignments between them during 1925 and 1926 and became close friends. But when Greer's four-year contract expired in 1927, he chose not to renew it, saying he was tired of always having to think in terms of black and white. He opened his own couture shop where stars sometimes bought clothes for their own and their film wardrobes. Over the years he did many more films but always on a freelance basis.

Travis Banton then became very powerful and a new contract signed in 1929 gave him absolute authority over actresses who now had no choice but to wear what he gave them. 'He was a god there' says Edith Head, 'nobody dared oppose

opposite
Claire West and Howard Greer: a scene from De Mille's *The Ten Commandments* (1923).

Howard Greer and Pola Negri working on *The Spanish Dancer* (1922).

him about anything, including the budgets'. But even prior to this contract, Banton had been very skillful in persuading actresses to adopt his styles and enjoy his clothes. In 1925 he tangled with Leatrice Joy over the length of her skirts in *The Dressmaker from Paris,* and then changed Florence Vidor's mind about her style of dress. She had thought of herself as very plain and condemned attempts to put her in high fashion clothes as a waste of time. As Banton said, 'She thought she could not wear them skillfully and that any old thing would do.' His lavish gowns for her in *The Grand Duchess and the Waiter* (1926) convinced her otherwise.

Banton had less success with Clara Bow. She enchanted Banton, but he found her complete lack of interest in fashion very saddening. She insisted on wearing high heels and ankle socks with every outfit, including bathing suits and evening gowns; she adorned his most elegant frocks with junk jewellery and stuck belts on them which ruined the straight lines of his dresses. Banton argued in vain that the high-society types that she was portraying in *Dancing Mothers* (1926) and *Children of Divorce* (1927) would not dress like that. When Clara began putting on a lot of weight, Banton gave up and turned her over to Edith Head.

Banton created the forerunners of the extreme helmets of the late twenties when he persuaded Evelyn Brent and Louise Brooks to wear cloche hats from which he had removed the face-shading brims as well as all other detail in order to show off their beautiful heads and necks.

However, his costumes for the great beauties of the twenties were just warming up exercises for Banton, whose chief fame rests on his uniquely elegant designs of the thirties. What set Banton apart from the other top designers of the period was his concentration on the female body which he draped in a simple manner that fully accentuated all of its natural beauties. He was fortunate that all of the Paramount stars of the 1930s had beautiful bodies and knew how to move superbly. Unlike Adrian at MGM, Banton did not have to create startling devices to distract attention from broad hips and sloping shoulders. Where Adrian would use sharp contrasts of black and white, Banton usually kept his designs to a close range of tones. His choice of ornamentation provided contrasting textures rather than contrasting colour values.

Banton's extraordinary perception found what was special in each woman, both in her figure and in her mind and he exploited these qualities. 'Travis only needed to have lunch with a girl once and he would know what she had that he could work with', observed a colleague, 'Carole Lombard was just a tootsie when she came to Paramount, but he saw things in her even she didn't know she had and his clothes transformed her.' Banton capitalized on Lombard's stance by giving her heavily beaded, bias cut evening gowns longer in the back and weighted to drag backwards, always moulded tightly against her thighs. Lombard's favourite gown was designed by Banton for *Love Before Breakfast* (1936), and had tightly draped black satin across her thighs with the added emphasis of a big bow on one side just below her hip.

As Lombard's career progressed, Banton's clothes helped her gain stature as a serious actress. He went beyond her good natured sexuality and stressed her intelligence and compassion. The sensual drapery continued in some dresses but in others was replaced by straight lines and stark simplicity. For the dramatic *Swing High, Swing Low* (1937) Banton designed several modest pastel frocks, well cut but devoid of any trimming save for some barely perceptible ruffles. With these went quiet little hats with bands under the brim to pare down Lombard's too high forehead. The Lombard clothes represent Banton's purest designing. Neither Lombard nor her directors ever imposed any ideas on him.

Travis Banton: Clara Bow in *The Saturday Night Kid* (1929).

Travis Banton: Carole Lombard models a
gown for *Now and Forever* (1934) for
Banton and his former employer,
Madame Frances.

She wore whatever he made, refused to pass approval on his sketches and did not see the dress until it was ready for the first fitting. She remained fiercely loyal to Banton and made it clear that she would not accept any other designer. The rest of Banton's stars were, in varying degrees, more difficult to deal with.

Claudette Colbert started making films for Paramount's New York studios in 1928, but Banton did not design for her until *The Man From Yesterday* (1932). Colbert had already acquired a knowledge of the cinematic craft, and with it, very certain ideas of how she should be dressed and photographed. She had arranged her own wardrobes for her early films herself, and when she met Banton, she did not want to give him any more freedom than she gave her cameramen, and issued him with a long list of materials and styles she would not wear. Fortunately Banton recognized and respected the intense perfectionism which touched all aspects of Colbert's work. Although he and everybody else thought her figure was perfect, he humoured Colbert when she insisted that her waist and hips were too thick and drew attention upward by baring her bosom in *Cleopatra* (1934) and *Torch Singer* (1933). When the Hays Office anti-cleavage rules of 1934 put a stop to this, Banton kept the eye up with an invention which became known in the business as the Colbert collar. Since Colbert thought her neck was too short and for this reason seldom wore shoulder length hair, Banton never closed her collar right at the base of her neck, but extended it down an inch or two while making the sides of the collar very wide, taking them to her shoulders in *Cleopatra* (see page 115).

Banton began experimenting with shoulder broadening lines and puffed sleeves on Colbert at the same time as Adrian began to broaden Joan Crawford's shoulders. Colbert wore a Letty Lynton dress in *The Gilded Lily* (1935) and was the first at Paramount to wear shoulder pads. Banton even put little pads into the shoulders of the otherwise authentic *Maid of Salem* (1938). Even though Colbert's beautiful legs had been the basis of her first fame on Broadway, she refused to expose them on the screen after her De Mille epics, and other than a very brief scene in a bathing suit in *Bluebeard's Eighth Wife* (1938) Banton had to keep her legs covered. Although Banton came to consider Colbert a close personal friend, they continued to fight over his designs.

Banton always had a good working relationship with Mae West. For Mae the formula was simple, 'Diamonds – lots of 'em' and huge hats, feather boas, fox stoles and vertical panels of light material or brilliants with darker side panels to slim her down. When Lombard and Colbert played comedy, they wore the same elegant clothes as in the dramas, but Mae's costumes were intended to be camp. Banton did six of her eight Paramount films, Head did one, and *Every Day's A Holiday* (1938) was designed by Elsa Schiaparelli. Mae sent a dress form to Paris for fittings but when the clothes arrived they did not fit and much reworking had to be done, so nobody tried another long-distance arrangement with Paris.

The star who made Banton's art immortal is Marlene Dietrich. The bizarre Josef von Sternberg vehicles for Dietrich inspired Banton's most imaginative creations and the continuing fascination with these pictures makes Banton's name known today. Banton was as much a part in the formation of the Dietrich image as cinematographer Lee Garmes, whose lighting created the classic Dietrich face, Sternberg who co-ordinated the whole effort with many ideas of his own, and Dietrich herself who took over on the films Sternberg did not direct.

Banton thought that Dietrich's figure though perfect for Lola in *The Blue Angel* in 1930, was too plump, and he started her on a regime of diet and exercise. With the figure that resulted and garbed in Banton's clothes, Dietrich became the sleekest siren of the age.

Travis Banton: Kay Francis in *Girls about Town* (1932); a perfect example of the slinky thirties posture.

While he was working with her on her first American film, *Morocco* (1930), Banton discovered the key to Dietrich's personality: her incredible discipline. Several of the dresses were not complete when shooting began and since Sternberg shot mostly in the evenings, Banton had to schedule fittings at midnight and work until dawn. Dietrich would arrive, pale and unsteady with exhaustion, but determined not to release the seamstresses until every miniscule wrinkle had been smoothed. Kay Francis and Carole Lombard both had the fashionable slinky, pelvis-thrust-forward posture of the era, but Dietrich's spine was always ramrod straight. Soon she was extremely slim and Banton began working to give her a softer quality. Her clothes would usually be fussier than any others he designed, with drapings of fabric and much use of fur and velvet that would be unflattering to a heavier figure. Sternberg apparently directed Banton to come up with something bizarre for the final scenes of *Dishonoured* (1931) for Banton produced a riot of contrasting textures that only Dietrich's personality and carriage could support. She wore a coat with an enormous trimming of monkey fur at the collar and cuffs, a small hat entirely covered in feathers, with a long black veil with white dots and a frilly lace jabot.

For *The Scarlet Empress* (1934), Banton gave Dietrich very ornate gowns with wide hoop skirts. He also enveloped her and the rest of the cast in fur, upon the orders of Paramount head, Adolph Zukor, who had once been a furrier and thought this might help the fur trade. Fortunately it was also highly appropriate to the mood of the film.

The final Sternberg-Dietrich film, *The Devil is a Woman* (1935), contained the weirdest and most beautiful garments Banton designed in his career. Even more inventive with the Spanish motifs than *The Scarlet Empress* had been with the Russian, *The Devil is a Woman* made constant use of seductive diagonal lines. In several changes, the 45 degree angle of Dietrich's hat was repeated in a drape that crossed from her left shoulder to her right hip. Banton found more textures than ever to work with: black satin ruffles dotted with occasional and enormous sequins, red and white carnations grouped in Dietrich's hair, lace panels on her stockings, abundant fringing. There were enormous combs in her hair, cocked at the 45 degree angle, and spitcurls on her forehead.

To what extent Sternberg himself designed the Dietrich costumes is as hard a question to answer as how much he photographed the films. Certainly the decision to clothe Dietrich's Concha Perez in such exaggerated, almost comic terms was his as well as many other specific ideas. The use of the 45° angle was also his idea. 'I placed those hats on her head myself every morning' he would recall in 1969, 'but Marlene always made herself up . . .' She put on her eyebrows also at a 45° angle. However, the bulk of the creative work was nonetheless Banton's.

The last two Banton films for Dietrich, *Desire* (1936) and *Angel* (1937) were both modern dress stories calling for 'straight' clothes and Banton handled them both alike, alternating between clothes that played up Dietrich's discipline and others that softened her, with an emphasis on the latter. For *Desire* he gave her a very fully draped white chiffon gown with the material on the bodice bunched up into a puff under her left jaw.* A device like this could have been disastrous on even the most slender of women but Dietrich was so extraordinary that it worked beautifully. For another scene Banton put a big organdie bow at the neck of a simple white wool dress. Though barely visible, the bow softened the neckline and added bulk.

The disciplined outfit for *Desire* was a very masculine suit, with a shoulder-padded blue blazer, a man's white shirt and a mid-calf white duck skirt. The

---

* Cameraman Charles Lang repeated the old maxim that pure white could not be photographed. Dietrich insisted that it must be and Lang found a way with lighting and filters to reduce the halation to a faint glow which intensified the softening qualities of the chiffon making her even more beautiful.

suit for *Angel* was much softer: the fabric was a soft white wool with a rough
finish and there was no padding in the shoulders. A more severe costume for
Angel was a two piece evening suit with yellow beads and red and green cabou-
chons. Again the shoulder seam was right at the shoulder line and the sleeves
were widened with padding. The cost of this one costume, including a fur trimmed scarf that was hardly used, was $8,000. It ended Banton's association with
Marlene Dietrich in a blaze of glory, for they did not work together again.

Banton's work was of almost uniformly high quality and he dressed the other
Paramount actresses of the thirties with beauty, taste and restraint. However,

opposite
Travis Banton: Marlene Dietrich in
Desire (1936).

Edith Head: a costume sketch for Greta Nissen in *The Wanderer* (1925).

always a highly troubled person, Banton's behaviour became increasingly erratic as the 1930s wore on. He drank heavily and sometimes would spend days on end riding around on the Los Angeles streetcars. Other times he turned up inexplicably in San Francisco and Chicago. It was through his sheer brilliance that he managed to hold his job as long as he did. After one absence Banton came into his office very early and sketching furiously, designed a whole picture in one morning. He grew increasingly arrogant. When he was warned, he told the studio he would be glad to be fired so that he could make more money free-lancing and doing collections like Greer. So when Banton's contract expired in March 1938, the studio decided it no longer needed him. Dietrich and West had left and Head, working for a fraction of the salary Banton demanded, could handle the rest.* In a letter to Natalie Visart, Carole Lombard wrote, 'About Travis – well as you know, the past year he has been a very bad boy and the studio just got fed up with it. That was that. He's having a little trouble getting something else. I don't think he appreciated his soft spot.' At the rumours that Head had somehow conspired to get Banton's job, Lombard exploded, 'Nonsense. She loved him as much as anybody, and if I ever make another picture at Paramount I want Edie to do all my clothes.' By the autumn of 1938 Edith Head was Paramount's chief designer.

Head's career had begun in the summer of 1923, when Howard Greer advertised in the newspaper for sketch artists to help on De Mille's *The Golden Bed*. She had decided to study drawing so that she could eventually earn more money by teaching it, but with typical thoroughness, she enrolled at two schools, and seeing Greer's ad, borrowed drawings from her fellow students, signed them 'Head' and applied for the job. Howard Greer declared her the most versatile artist he had ever seen and hired her.

Head's sketching was really very poor at first and Greer soon caught on to her ruse. Nonetheless, he kept her on because she was hardworking and bright without displaying enough tangible talent to pose a threat to him. She became assistant to Greer and Banton, and frequently dressed the male and supporting female characters out of stock wardrobe. When Greer left in 1927, Head began designing some films on her own while continuing to assist Banton and taking over some of Banton's more difficult actresses, including Nancy Carroll whose tantrums infuriated Banton. Once, after Head and her fitter had spent hours perfecting a dress, Carroll calmly ripped it to shreds in front of them.

There was no fanfare when Head became Paramount's head designer. The studio had become the least glamorous of Hollywood's major lots and although her name was on a staggering total of credits each year, never less than thirty-five films a year between 1937 and 1942, the majority were the new B pictures Paramount was pushing under the management of William LeBaron. 'You could just make it if you worked every day until midnight and weekends' says Head, 'in some ways it was easier than today because we knew way in advance what pictures we were going to do and who would be in them. Dottie Lamour, Martha Raye, Frances Farmer; these girls were all under contract and I made many pictures with them so I knew their figures, their likes and dislikes. The studio had an enormous stock of fabrics, everything I could possibly need. I never had to shop very much. We had some tough directors on the Bs but generally they weren't as involved in the clothes as the later directors.'

Edith Head: Dorothy Lamour in *Masquerade in Mexico* (1945). This shows how nude souffle looked to the naked eye: invisible where it fits snugly, but all too visible where it drooped as under the arm. This kind of lace over souffle remained fashionable throughout the war years.

Among the A pictures were several with Madeleine Carroll, and Irene Dunne's *Invitation to Happiness* (1939) gave Head a rare opportunity to prove that she could do period costumes, even recent period, with complete accuracy provided the star was willing to wear it. The dripping hemlines, low waists and cloches of

* Colbert used Head only once in *Zaza* (1938). Irene, who had been making her personal wardrobe, now did her Paramount films while Head did the supporting cast.

Edith Head: Barbara Stanwyck in *The Lady Eve* (1941); one of the first of many dresses Head would design for Stanwyck along the same basic lines.

the late twenties all seemed absurd in 1939 but Dunne felt this look would make the picture more realistic and Head jumped at the chance to provide it.

The star who finally made Head an overnight success after eighteen years of hard work was Barbara Stanwyck in *The Lady Eve* (1941). Until then, Stanwyck had usually been cast in roles that did not call for high fashion clothes. Designers found Stanwyck a warm and appealing person, but indifferent towards her clothes. Slender with perfect posture, Stanwyck's figure was better than those of most of her contemporaries although she had a long waist and low-slung derrière. Previous designers coped with this by cheating her waistline up and then hiding the rest under full skirts even when full skirts were unfashionable. But Head was determined to raise Stanwyck's waist and keep her in straight skirts. She succeeded, through the invention of a self-belt that was wider in the back than the front, and through increased fullness over the bust and sleeves to divert the eye. Aware of the topicality of anything Latin-American in the final months before America entered the war, Head cleverly used Spanish motifs on much of *The Lady Eve* wardrobe even though the locale of the story, on board a ship, was not really Spanish.

The results were sensational. Latin-American clothes swept the country. Head had launched a major trend, and for the first time, Stanwyck was regarded as a clothes-horse and she loved it. She praised Head in every interview she gave and

insisted that Head design all her future films. In the next seven years, Head was loaned to Goldwyn, Columbia, Universal, Warner Brothers, Hunt Stromberg and Enterprise for Stanwyck pictures. Until the advent of the New Look after the war, Stanwyck persuaded Head to repeat the *Lady Eve* look time and again.

The rapport between Stanwyck and Head was not surprising since they are both hard-working and completely dedicated to their professions, but Head could get along well with anybody concerned with making a film. She explains, 'When I've designed a square neckline and a star wants it round, I don't argue with her', but it goes further than that. Producers and directors find her flexible and versatile; cameramen and sound recorders, choreographers and art directors find her sympathetic to their problems; and since technicians from all the crafts vote for the Academy Awards, her close collaboration with all members of a crew is one of the reasons she has won so many Oscars.

Unlike most of the other designers, Head has never done couture or wholesale work. Her designs work only in the context of a certain actress in a certain film. Recalling the Head costumes for her two Oscar winning roles in *To Each His Own* (1946) and *The Heiress* (1949) Olivia de Havilland says, 'Every dress was perfect. Just putting them on, I became these women and I knew right where they were in the stories. Edith even came to New York with me before *The Heiress* and we studied the underwear at the Brooklyn Museum so it would be absolutely authentic.'

Edith Head: a still from *For Whom the Bell Tolls* (1943) with Ingrid Bergman.

Head fights more over characterization in clothes than style. 'I wanted Edith to make me a knitted shawl for my first scene with the fish merchant in *The Heiress*', relates de Havilland, 'because Walter Plunkett had given us knitted things in *Gone With The Wind* and they emphasized Melanie's modesty and poverty. I thought a knitted shawl would point up Catherine Sloper's modesty in *The Heiress*. Well, Edith didn't agree. She said Catherine was well-to-do and wouldn't wear anything knitted, no matter how modest. But she went ahead and made it up. When I saw the test, I knew she was right. It cost Edith on her budget but she was very decent about it and used the shawl on another actress.'

The fortunes of Paramount improved tremendously during the Second World War and Head began getting highly prestigious assignments and important loanouts. After working with Ginger Rogers in *The Major and the Minor* (1942), she accompanied Rogers to RKO, where she also dressed Ingrid Bergman in *For Whom the Bell Tolls* (1943). She gave Bergman an old shirt and pants that she had found in the extra men's wardrobe. When word of these used garments reached David O. Selznick he was furious, so Head made new ones and then laboriously bleached and redyed them until they looked as worn as the originals.

Head was also assigned to Veronica Lake when she came to Paramount. Lake arrived with her hair in pigtails, wearing a beret and a pleated skirt and looking

Veronica Lake as a siren.

generally like an eleven year old schoolgirl. Transforming her into a slinky siren was another of Head's successes. The Lake hairstyle, created by a Paramount hairdresser, made the initial impact, and Head followed it with sultry gold lamé and beaded gowns. Lake's little girl qualities could also have been counteracted by her admirable bosom but the Hays Office anti-cleavage rules were still in force and Head had to keep it covered up. Head also had to cover up the fact that Lake was very pregnant while *Sullivan's Travels* (1943) was being filmed.

However Head could not handle everything, so several other designers were brought in for various assignments. Cecil B. De Mille had always brought in outside designers for his films, which relied on splendid costumes for part of their effect.

The costumes for *The Sign of the Cross* (1932) were the work of Mitchell Leisen, and while the Paramount staff did *Four Frightened People* (1934), Milo Anderson was borrowed from Warners for *This Day and Age* (1934). Leisen refused to come back for *Cleopatra* (1934) and De Mille felt the staff of designers needed somebody tougher than Banton to guide the overall effort. In the end Banton did dress Claudette Colbert – superbly, and the rest were handled by a committee of talented designers including Ralph Jester, Shannon Rogers, Vicki and Natalie Visart. Thousands of costumes had to be made as cheaply as possible. 'We made

left
Natalie Visart with Barbara Stanwyck on
Union Pacific (1938). Stanwyck's dress
is actually a modernized, female version
of the costume Visart designed for Joel
McCrea, adapted here for publicity
purposes.

right
Natalie Visart: a costume test of Paulette
Goddard in De Mille's *Northwest
Mounted Police* (1940). De Mille always
insisted that women wear high heels, so
Goddard has concealed wedgies in her
moccasins. This costume satisfied no one
until Charles Chaplin suggested removing
the fringe from the skirt.

sleazy little bras and skirts on elastics so they could fit anybody', remembers
Shannon Rogers.

Most of the *Cleopatra* committee worked on *The Crusades* (1936), but after
that, Natalie Visart carried most of the load alone. She recalls, 'We had a
Technicolor consultant on *Northwest Mounted Police* (1940) who told De Mille
he could not put red and orange in the same scene. De Mille sat and fumed for a
moment and then yelled, "Well, it's too bad the good lord up in heaven didn't
have a Technicolor consultant when he made apples and oranges!"'

After Visart retired in 1945, De Mille returned to the committee system.
Unconquered (1947) was worked on by Madame Karinska and Gwen Wakeling.
And Wakeling, Head, Dorothy Jeakins and Elois Jenssen worked on *Samson and
Delilah* (1949) which won them the second Oscar for Colour Costume Design (see
page 123). After 1949 Head dressed the female principals in all De Mille's films,
though Jeakins, Miles White, John Jensen and Ralph Jester collaborated at
various times. 'We had meetings to make sure everything was going together
but there really wasn't much point. If De Mille liked it it went in regardless of
any good reasons we might have.'

A Broadway designer, Raoul Pene du Bois, was also brought in, and designed costumes and sets for six films in four years. Three of these, *Lady in the Dark* (1944) *Frenchman's Creek* (1944), and *Kitty* (1945), were directed by Mitchell Leisen. With his design background, he was usually loudly dissatisfied with any costumes designed for his films. Characteristically self-effacing, Head bore the abuse with a smile, but du Bois did not and consequently the three films were riddled with quarrels. Leisen haunted the workrooms, reworking the garments until they bore little resemblance to the original du Bois designs. *Lady in the Dark*, Paramount's biggest fashion picture ever, is a mass of unresolved controversy over who designed what. However, in the most important dream sequence costume, Ginger Rogers' dress with the mink skirt lined with red and gold brilliants was designed by Head, working under instructions from Leisen.

About the same time, Mary Kay Dodson, a Beverly Hills couturiere was given a design contract. Her first task was to dress the cast of *Practically Yours* (1943) while Greer costumed Colbert. Then she shared two films with Head, after which she received many prestigious assignments, but by 1950 there was not enough work for two full-time designers, so her contract was not renewed.

on page 66
Edith Head and Mitchell Leisen: Ginger Rogers in the famous mink dress from *Lady in the Dark* (1943).

on page 67
Mary Kay Dobson: Marlene Dietrich in *Golden Earring* (1947). This costume was a compromise between the ideas of the designer and the star. When Dietrich arrived from Europe, she proceeded to remake all the costumes, because she said she knew real gypsies in France, and how they dressed.

Raoul Pene du Bois: a still from *Frenchmen's Creek* (1944) with Joan Fontaine. The film was a major job of historical costuming.

Edith Head: Gloria Swanson in *Sunset Boulevard* (1950).

If the films were fewer, Head's opportunities for characterization in costume design were generally better in the 1950s. *Sunset Boulevard* (1950) showed great restraint. Although the person Gloria Swanson played lived in a twenties house in a world of silent cinema, she wore contemporary clothes, hair and make-up. There were exotic and bizarre touches, but none were carried to the extent of being camp. 'Gloria wasn't a fan of the full skirts and petticoats of the New Look so we used straight skirts and drapery that showed her beautiful thighs. I was dressing a star as a star and I've never had a picture that was smoother or more enjoyable.'

A Place in the Sun, made in 1949 but not released until 1951, showed Head could foresee future fashion. She designed a strapless evening gown for Elizabeth Taylor that was the last word in fashion when the film was finally released. The bodice was covered with white violets and the skirt was made of miles of white tulle over green satin. Paramount displayed the dress in department stores around the country and so many copies were sold that a fashion writer commented: 'Go to any party this summer and you'll see at least ten of them.' For George Stevens' *Shane* (1953), she designed the costumes for Alan Ladd and Van Heflin as well as Jean Arthur, a rare occasion during the fifties when she was asked to dress men, although she had plenty of experience of doing so from her earliest days at Paramount.

Many of Edith Head's assignments in the 1950s were for producer Hal Wallis. Between *Love Letters* (1945) and *Rooster Cogburn* (1975), Head has designed

Edith Head: Elizabeth Taylor and Montgomery Clift in *A Place in the Sun* (1951).

nearly all of his productions, a total of over sixty films. Making relatively few films per year, Wallis could pay very close attention to their every aspect. 'He hated the Adrian kind of thing where Joan Crawford would be clerking in a dime-store, dressed to the teeth,' says Head. 'If I had any fashion innovations, I would use them somewhere else, not in a Wallis picture because he will never allow clothes to compete with performance. In the Westerns, I kept taking period detail off the women until the clothes belonged to no date at all.* Other period films however, especially *Summer and Smoke* (1962), had no expense spared to make the clothes accurate, even fussy because it helped the character-izations.'

Head has enjoyed another long, happy collaboration with Alfred Hitchcock. Although she had designed *Notorious* (1946), it was at Ingrid Bergman's request and Head did not really get to know Hitchcock and his views on the psycho-logical impact of colours until *Rear Window* (1954). 'Hitchcock explained it to me, "It's really very simple, Edith. Keep the colours quiet unless we need some dramatic impact." He likes eau de nile green, greys. When we started *Vertigo*

Edith Head: Grace Kelly in *To Catch a Thief* (1955).

* This is especially evident in *The Furies* (1949), *The Sons of Katie Elder* (1963) and *Rooster Cogburn* (1975).

(1958) I went to Kim Novak's dressing room and she said, "Dear Edith, how nice to meet you. I must tell you the only things I never wear are tailored suits, anything grey, and black pumps. My shoes must be nude to match my stockings." I said, "Well, right here in the script, it says a grey tailored suit and black pumps." So I went to Hitch and he said, "Don't worry Edith." and she wore the grey and it was never mentioned again. I did make a black and emerald green satin evening ensemble for the scene in the restaurant because it was an inportant story point. Both of the characters Kim played wore green, it was the colour of death. But other than colours, Hitchcock gives you a lot of room for your own ideas.'

Hitchcock's *To Catch a Thief* (1955) with Grace Kelly is Head's all time favourite film and certainly her most glamorous. The elegant drapery of the pale blue chiffon with the massive 'imitation' diamond necklace were the perfect metaphor for the classic Hitchcock woman, passionate under a cool exterior, while the balloon skirted gold lamé ballgown and wig proved Head could conjure up the traditional Hollywood splendour. 'Hitch had said, "I want absolutely no strong colours". So I used the palest pastels all the way through so that when she appeared in the gold, the climax was all the more effective.'

Head has also worked closely with director George Seaton who has assigned her to most of his films in the last twenty-five years. In *The Country Girl* (1954) Grace Kelly had to wear the drabbest possible costumes. Seaton recounts, 'We were all worried that Grace would be too beautiful but Edie got her a couple of dresses that made her feel plain and depressed just to put them on.'

The 1950s brought a new breed of actresses into the Paramount fold, and the versatile Head changed her techniques to accommodate them. Besides being a brilliant performer, Audrey Hepburn had the kind of rail-thin, broadshouldered, miniscule-waisted figure all designers fantasize about when they make their sketches. Head exploited this figure in *Roman Holiday* (1953) and *Sabrina* (1954): ignoring her usual expertise at camouflage, she did not envelope Hepburn's long neck in chokers, turtle necks or furs, did not hide her collarbone under swathings of chiffon and did not pad her bustline. Even her legs, muscular from years as a dancer, were played up in short, tight toreador pants and her big feet got bigger in flat Capezios. The pants and shoes swept the country.

1955 brought Shirley MacLaine to Paramount. Although her first film, *Artists and Models* (1955) brought a chance to design a glamorous bat costume, most of her later ones kept the clothes low-key. Then in 1964, Head was lent to Fox for *What a Way to Go*, which proved to be the most extravagant picture of her career. The plot had MacLaine recounting her six marriages, each episode a parody of some film genre. One spoofed producer Ross Hunter's lavish films: MacLaine was enveloped in pale pink complete with pink fox muff and a towering pink wig. There was a red patent leather gown held together with liquid cement and a spectacular white beaded number with décolletage plunged to the waist. The producer, director and star agreed that the focal point of the film should be MacLaine's shapely and very long legs. Therefore just about every skirt was tight, shoes were backless whenever possible, and bathing suits and dance costumes were cut high on the hip. Publicity alleged that Head had a million dollar budget and the result was the greatest tour de force of her career.

Edith Head's style became somewhat more flamboyant in the 1960s, in keeping with the times. She who had always foresworn bust padding now became expert at it, and in her hands actresses blossomed forth with the most unexpected cleavages. By now most films were in colour, and there were more comedies and more high fashion.

Edith Head: Shirley MacLaine wearing the 'Diamond Dress' in *What a Way to Go* (1964).

Edith Head: Audrey Hepburn in *Sabrina* (1954); the dress does nothing to conceal her long neck, protruding collar bones or large feet.

Paramount had not lent Head out since 1950, but in 1957 she did *Witness for the Prosecution* for her old friends Marlene Dietrich and Billy Wilder, and was borrowed more frequently in the sixties. She went to Columbia for *Pepe* (1960), an extravaganza which took place all over Mexico and required 2,500 designs; Natalie Wood and Shirley MacLaine pictures took her to every studio in town; she was borrowed increasingly by Universal, where longtime Paramount colleagues Hitchcock, Wallis and Seaton went in the sixties. When Paramount was purchased in 1967, the studio was shut down and Edith Head left her home of forty-four years. 'We saw it coming and we all felt so sorry for Edith', says Howard Shoup, who was working on *Hotel* with her at Warners at the time, 'but the minute Paramount shut down, she announced she was signing with Universal. She had been planning it all the time and she never let on.' 'Edith *never* tells.' adds Lucille Ball.

Since then, Paramount has had no contract designer, but has produced more films notable for their costumes than any other studio. Theoni V. Aldrich did *The Great Gatsby* and Anthea Sylbert did *Chinatown* (both 1974). In 1975, four of the five Oscar nominations were for Paramount films and Head returned once, for Elizabeth Taylor's *Ash Wednesday* (1973), the only instance of highly glamorous contemporary clothes in a recent American-produced film.

Warner Brothers Wit

on previous page
Orry Kelly: Kay Francis in *Stolen Holiday* (1937).

Orry Kelly: Kay Francis in *Mandalay* (1935).

For most of the 1920s Warner Brothers was the poorest of the major studios, and apart from the lush John Barrymore pictures, there was little for a designer to do. In the 1930s the Warner lot, with its tough gangster movies and grim social realism, might appear a poor berth for a talented costume designer, but Busby Berkeley musicals, costume dramas and glamorous vehicles were all produced at the same time, and costumed by a designer considered to be one of the best, certainly the wittiest, in the business, Orry Kelly.

Warners' fortunes changed and their costume design history began with the enormous success of *The Jazz Singer* in 1927. They built a new movie palace in Hollywood and employed Earl Luick as a stage and film designer. Then they bought First National in 1929 and brought over Edward Stevenson as well. The two designers worked amicably together for a year, but Stevenson left in a huff over his lack of screen credit in 1931 and Luick left to go to Fox in 1932. This left the studio that had just lured two big stars, Kay Francis and Ruth Chatterton, away from Paramount with no suitable designer to dress them.

Into the breach came Orry Kelly in 1932. He made his formal debut on Chatterton's *The Rich are Always With Us* (1932), which also featured a young Bette Davis.

Within a year, he was joined by Milo Anderson, certainly Hollywood's youngest designer. Anderson's sketches had so impressed Samuel Goldwyn that he gave him the job of designing *The Kid From Spain* (1932) when he was only seventeen and still at school! That film introduced him to Busby Berkeley who took him along when he moved to Warner Brothers for *42nd Street* (1932). Kelly dressed the principals, but Anderson did most of the numbers because he best understood Berkeley's ideas.

Kelly was cordial with Anderson and although he took his pick of the assignments, he let Anderson have several top ones too. Kelly always dressed Bette Davis and Kay Francis while Anderson specialized in Olivia de Havilland, Errol Flynn and later Ida Lupino and Ann Sheridan. The general tone of the studio was set by Kelly and followed by Anderson: utter simplicity and high fashion without theatricality. Kelly saw that many of the less successful designers at other studios were copying Adrian's formula of using black against white and lots of glitter. Although Kelly had a great knack for arresting effects, his desire to be unique was even greater. He stuck to the middle greys as much as possible and used dull-finished wools, velvets and chiffons.

Kelly found his ideal subject for pure fashion in Kay Francis. The costumes he created did not have to conceal anything in her figure and the characters she played were so interchangeable they usually had no bearing on the designs. Her walk combined sex appeal with authority and Kelly played this up with simplicity and the constant use of vertical lines to accentuate her slim hips and long legs. She was very impressed when he took a golf skirt pattern with two inverted pleats in the back, dropped it to the floor and made it into an evening dress. He gave her a pleated white toga and white wig for *I Found Stella Parish* (1935), but there was no such nonsense when she played Florence Nightingale in *The White Angel* (1936). Her lack of bosom or defined waistline made Francis a little unlikely for hour-glass silhouettes, but by using ruffles and corsets Kelly gave her a lovely nineteenth century image in *I Loved a Woman* and *The House on 56th Street* (both 1933). When the studio sought to humiliate her into breaking her contract by putting her in B pictures Kelly risked trouble by insisting on designing all her films until her contract ended.

Kelly also got along well with Chatterton, despite her proclivity towards 1915 era georgette ruffles. He was very fond of Joan Blondell although he found her figure difficult, 'she's too rounded, clothes only clutter her up'. Very handy with a needle and thread, Blondell sometimes altered her own garments after Kelly's final fitting to better show off her assets.

on pages 76 and 77
Milo Anderson: the closing number from Busby Berkeley's *42nd Street* (1932).

Orry Kelly and Josephine Hutchinson in a publicity shot for *Oil for the Lamps of China* (1935).

The greatest challenge to Warners' designers was Bette Davis whom Kelly costumed from 1933 to 1946. She referred to him as her 'right hand' and depended upon his clothes to help her define her roles, but as much as she sought out his advice, she often disagreed with it. Kelly was as adept at debate as she was, but they remained devoted.

Davis' supposed lack of physical beauty was a matter of great concern to the studio in the early years of her career. Her hair was bleached, then covered with a platinum wig, and make-up drastically altered her face in *Fashions of 1934*. Much of this artifice became unnecessary by the late 1930s, as her face grew increasingly popular with the public, but her figure problems remained. Her neck was long and broad and Kelly usually had to design all kinds of high collars, sometimes using ruffles or big bows. In the 1940s her shoulder length hair made her neck seem less long, but Davis liked to change her appearance in each modern dress film, so that despite the same voice and face, each role was individual. In *Now Voyager* (1942) she not only kept her hair swept up throughout, but Kelly gave her the kind of v necklines usually used to make short necks seem longer!

She would wear any kind of corset necessary for her period pictures because she strove for accuracy and the discomfort helped her find the proper frame of reference. For her modern roles, however, she refused to wear any garments that

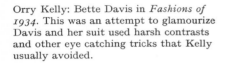

Orry Kelly: Bette Davis in *Fashions of 1934*. This was an attempt to glamourize Davis and her suit used harsh contrasts and other eye catching tricks that Kelly usually avoided.

were uncomfortable or constrictive and that included most brassières, with the result that her large bust hung unfashionably low. Kelly frequently demanded of his very capable assistant, Leah Rhodes, 'Give me some way to break her bosom.' Sometimes he managed to build some support into the front of the dress, but more often he camouflaged Davis' matronly look with full sleeves and the addition of bulk higher up. *The Little Foxes* (1941) (for which he was loaned to Goldwyn with Davis) was produced during the brief period when some display of cleavage in period films was allowed, and Kelly designed a beautiful white lace evening dress and a corset that restructured Davis magnificently.

Hal Wallis, the production chief, made Kelly's work more difficult because he meddled constantly. Hardly a slave to fashion, Davis wanted to be fashionable to be convincing as the rich heroines of *Dark Victory* (1939) and *The Great Lie* (1941). But although full and flared skirts had returned by the late thirties, Wallis vetoed them, as well as the hats of the period with even the simplest spill on to the forehead. Wallis also meddled in period costumes. He wanted Davis to wear much smaller farthingales in *The Private Lives of Elizabeth and Essex* (1939) than would have been correct. In the end Davis wore small hoops under her skirt for the tests, and once those had been approved by Wallis, she wore the correct size hoops for the actual filming.

Orry Kelly: Bette Davis in *Dark Victory* (1939). The cap makes a story point and is repeated several times in the film.

Milo Anderson and Olivia de Havilland work on *Captain Blood* (1936).

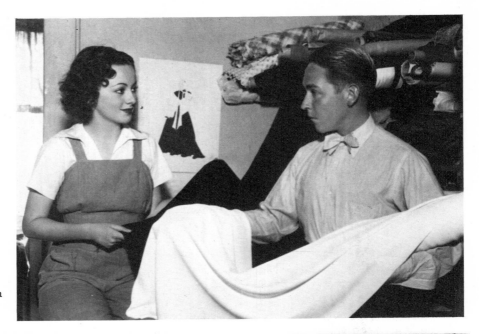

Orry Kelly and Milo Anderson: Bette Davis, Vincent Price, Henry Daniels, Olivia de Havilland and Donald Crisp in *The Private Lives of Elizabeth and Essex* (1939).

Wallis also vetoed a full skirt designed by Kelly for Olivia de Havilland in *It's Love I'm After* (1938). Kelly designed a few films for de Havilland, but the majority were done by Milo Anderson. 'I loved the romanticism and grace of his costumes. He seemed to get the same quality in the modern ones. When there was no characterization to work with, Milo used my personality. I think he captured me better than any other designer. I always did research on my own and once I came across a dress which had an ivy trimming which I suggested for *They Died with Their Boots On* (1941). I wouldn't have dared suggest anything to Kelly!'

Anderson designed some costumes for Davis when Kelly was away in Australia and the Army, including the pivotal red (actually brown for the camera) satin ball gown for *Jezebel* (1938), though Kelly had done the rest of the film quite brilliantly before he left. Hal Wallis also assigned Anderson to Marlene Dietrich for *Manpower* (1940), 'She was charming but difficult. Everytime she wanted me to do something I thought was wrong, she'd say "Well Irene does it for me." About a year later, Irene called me up and said "Why did you do that?" Now she keeps saying, "Well, Milo did it for me. . . ." '

Milo Anderson: Olivia de Havilland in the ivy-leaf trimmed dress in *They Died with their Boots on* (1942).

Howard Shoup and Ann Sheridan at a
fitting *c.* 1939.

Orry Kelly: Bette Davis in *Jezebel* (1938).
Although a period costume, the lines
were as carefully worked out to flatter
Davis as any modern dress. The chain
and the top of the bow create a definite
horizontal line to shorten her neck, while
the vertical ends of the ribbon and the
careful placement of the ruffles diminish
her bosom.

As productions became more lavish in the late 1930s, the work load became so
great that Hal Wallis employed a third designer, Howard Shoup, to handle the
B pictures. Kelly clearly resented Shoup's arrival. 'We need him like a hole in the
head' he groused, but perhaps suspected his own position was in jeopardy.
Having behaved contemptuously towards Ann Sheridan while she was unknown,
he wanted to design all her films when she became famous, although she wanted
to continue with Shoup and Anderson.

However, Kelly's skill continued to impress during the early forties. The
enormous success of *Casablanca* (1942), coupled with the simple construction of
Kelly's jumper for Ingrid Bergman made it one of the standard styles of the war
years. 'I wish I had a dime for every time that's been copied', he said. In 1940 he
also designed what became one of his trademarks – the dropped waistline. There
was a self belt at the normal waistline with the material below clinging tightly to
the hips, with the gathers beginning at the hips' fullest point. The belt kept it
from looking too 1920s, yet there was the advantage of a full skirt without bulk
at the waist. Davis and de Havilland both wore it several times.

Halfway through work on Bette Davis' *Old Acquaintance* (1942) Kelly was
drafted, and Leah Rhodes finished the film. Kelly came back a few months later,

Milo Anderson: a costume test of Olivia de Havilland in *Gold is Where You Find It* (1938). De Havilland played an early Californian orchard worker. Interesting details include the way part of the skirt is drawn up and the flat shoes.

but the studio had changed, everybody was satisfied with Anderson and Rhodes, and aside from the Davis films, Kelly was no longer needed. He began work on *Doughgirls*, but a dispute arose. As far as the studio was concerned it was the final straw and Kelly was fired. *Doughgirls* was re-assigned to Anderson, and *Saratoga Trunk* to Leah Rhodes. 'I never wanted to be a designer on my own because I couldn't argue like Orry did', she said. 'But Ingrid Bergman was so sweet it got so that she initialled the sketches, hardly looking at them. When I wanted a fitting, she said, "What's the use, they always fit perfectly."'

Kelly managed to return to Warners to make *Mr Skeffington* (1944), but only because the studio was giving Bette Davis everything she wanted. The film was Kelly's finest achievement in characterization. It covered the years from 1914 to 1935 and the design was uncompromisingly accurate. Fanny Skeffington's dress progressed gradually from slightly overdone Lady Duff Gordon in 1914 to the grotesque matron in the country club in 1935, by which time she has completely separated her look from conventional fashion. 'I never knew Bette to be concerned with looking good per se', says Vincent Sherman the director 'only with interpreting the character as she saw her. Kelly always talked the clothes over with me as well as Bette and I felt he got it just right.'

opposite
Orry Kelly: Bette Davis and Gail Sondergaard in *The Letter* (1940); Davis' gown features Kelly's trademark of a dropped waistline with a self sash. Sondergaard's costumes were redesigned by Kelly because she insisted the character should be more dignified than the stereotype Chinese prostitute.

Leah Rhodes: Ingrid Bergman in two costumes for *Saratoga Trunk* (1946). The hat was eventually not used. The plaid was pieced together from scraps at the ends of bolts because of wartime shortages, and there was barely enough for the trimming.

opposite
Edith Head: Bette Davis' first New Look
wardrobe, for *June Bride* (1948).

Edith Head: Barbara Stanwyck in *My
Reputation* (1945); this gown is a variation
on the *Lady Eve* dress of 1941.

on page 88
Sheila O'Brien: Joan Crawford in *Harriet
Craig* (1950, Columbia). For the first time
in her career, Crawford's clothes did not
seem bizarre or overdone. This was partly
because, once she had given up her
shoulder pads, the lines of the 1950s
flattered her, partly because her roles
dictated it, and partly because O'Brien
was very strong willed and fought to
tone down Crawford's image.

on page 89
William Travilla: Errol Flynn in *Don
Juan* (1948), in the highly fictionalized
Renaissance costumes.

The studio decided to obtain a well-known couturier in 1945 and hired Bernard Newman. His second fling in pictures was more disastrous than his first (at RKO) and ended by 1947. Bette Davis agreed to work with him on *Deception* (1946). She was pregnant and he did not conceal it very well. Clad in a bathrobe for one angry scene, she was forced to keep her arms folded all the way through in order to add enough bulk to her upper torso to conceal the bulk below.

Newman began work with Joan Crawford on *Humoresque* (1946). The previous year Crawford had made *Mildred Pierce* and had hated the way she looked, but had been in no position to do anything about it. But she had won an Oscar for her performance and so could now dictate to the designer. After several weeks and two complete wardrobes, there was still not a single garment she felt she could wear. In desperation, she brought in one of her own dresses, a white beaded evening gown with enormously padded shoulders which her dressmaker, Sheila O'Brien, had designed and made to Crawford's specifications. O'Brien tells the story, 'With those pads her shoulders measured the same as Clark Gable's. The producer was desperate, and was saying, "I'd give anything to get her out of those shoulder pads", so I got a scheme: every night after the whole crew had gone home, I'd take apart the whole shoulder seam, remove $\frac{1}{8}$ inch of the pad and remake the sleeve. Since it was done so gradually, she never noticed.'

O'Brien designed all Crawford's pictures for the next ten years, except *Torch Song* (1952) which was done by Helen Rose. The New Look had little effect on Crawford, she lengthened and widened her skirts, but kept her shoulder pads until well into the 1950s. O'Brien's favourite assignment was *The Damned Don't Cry* (1951) because 'the character changed from a factory worker to a very sophisticated lady.' O'Brien went on to found the Designers Guild in 1953.

William Travilla joined the Warners staff in 1945. His best work was done for *The Adventures of Don Juan* (1948). Leah Rhodes and Marjorie Best were already working on it when he was brought in to redesign Errol Flynn's wardrobe because Flynn decided that he would not wear any more padded trunks or big ruffs. As Travilla says, 'I created a look that was mostly fictitious but Flynn liked it. Collars, which they didn't have in the Renaissance, or very small ruffs, no trunks, long jackets which covered his rump, no puffy sleeves. Marge Best was very good about it, she changed enough of the extras and small parts so that Flynn wouldn't stick out like a sore thumb.' The payroll now carried three designers instead of two but ever-thrifty Leah Rhodes economized in some ways, 'Those gold beads on Viveca Lindfor's blue dress were really just chains off of electric lights. I made her ruffs out of woven horsehair and pearls rather than cotton lace that gets dirty and has to be washed and restarched.' The three designers won the first Oscar for the Best Colour Costume Design.

Warners had been borrowing Edith Head from Paramount since 1942 to dress Barbara Stanwyck. In 1948 she dressed Bette Davis for *June Bride* as an impeccably dressed businesswoman. Davis liked the longer, fuller skirts of the New Look and she went along with the uncomfortable boned bodices and brassières because she knew that was what the character would wear.

Meanwhile Leah Rhodes and Milo Anderson continued to dress the big Warner stars of the early fifties, Doris Day and Jane Wyman. Rhodes remembers, 'Doris Day had a slight little bump in the line of her shoulder from the collar bone. After she cut her hair short, we were told to make sure it was always covered; all her bathing suits and evening dresses had to have straps at that place or a necklace.' Rhodes left in 1952 because, 'I was doing three or four pictures at once. I wanted to do fewer pictures and better.' And Anderson left in 1953 for wholesale designing and interior decorating, saying that the glamour had gone out of the business.

PRODUCTION TESTS
FOR
THE ADVENTURES OF DON JUAN 691
OF

V. LINDFORS   E. FLYNN
" QUEEN "   AS   " DON JUAN "

HEIGHT	EYES
WEIGHT	HAIR
AGE	DATE 9-25-47

| SHERMAN | POLITO |

| SCENE* | TAKE* |

REMARKS

opposite
Orry Kelly: Marilyn Monroe in a costume
of black souffle and beads from *Some
Like It Hot* (1959).

Although Warners now had Shoup and Moss Marby on hand, they used outside talent for their biggest design job for years, *A Star Is Born* (1954). From the beginning it was plagued with problems. Rumours flew about the $100,000 worth of costumes that were made and then not used because of changes in the script, changes in Garland's mind and drastic changes in her weight. Just who designed what is uncertain because Mary Ann Nyberg left halfway through. Jean-Louis, who replaced her, seems to have done most of the second half, including the black satin for the Academy Award ceremony and the gold brocade and fur fox for the 'This is Mrs Norman Maine' scene filmed when Garland was very thin.

She was thinner still when Irene Sharaff was brought in to design the many costumes for the added 'Born in a Trunk' sequence. Working within the highly stylized concept of the numbers, Sharaff created many optical illusions to improve Garland's figure.

Orry Kelly returned to Warners at the request of Rosalind Russell for *Auntie Mame* (1958), which shows his fanciful imagination. This side of his talent would be featured in most of his remaining films. It is evident in a costume which Marilyn Monroe adored in *Some Like It Hot* (1959). Made of nude souffle draped on the bias to lift her breasts and push her tummy in, and covered with jet and crystal beads, it was so slightly beaded over her breasts that her nipples were not covered and Billy Wilder had to light her with a single spot that left that area strategically in darkness. Marilyn Monroe wanted to make her other clothes more revealing, but Kelly argued it was wrong for the character. 'Sugar Kane is the kind of girl who will go so far and no further,' he argued.

Kelly had always had a famous vitriolic temper, and it did not cool with age. In 1959 he tried to have a public feud with Head via Hedda Hopper's newspaper column, but since Head would not reciprocate, it failed. When he worked with Shelly Winters on *The Chapman Report* (1962), and she decided not to have the fitting that Kelly had reluctantly gone to her trailer for, he became enraged. He grabbed the side of the trailer and shook it until the terrified Winters was forced to run outside!

Jack Warner and George Cukor both wanted Kelly to design *My Fair Lady* (1964) but there was nothing they could do because the deal with Lerner and Lowe stipulated Cecil Beaton.

Beaton's handling of the assignment was splendid, enormously publicized and inevitably Academy Awarded. Viewed today it has a perceptible early sixties flavour. Beaton complained about the lack of suitable women extras for the Ascot scene, but what he did to them, the fishtail eyeliner, the hair teased and lacquered (losing the charming fuzziness of the Belle Epoque), seems inaccurate and uninspired ten years later. Audrey Hepburn's Ascot hat was magnificent in the audacity of its size and skill of construction but her other costumes are somewhat overly simplified.

Kelly died on 27 February 1964 of cancer, although Shoup says the real cause was 'a broken heart over losing *My Fair Lady*'.

Shoup had now become the longest tenured of the Warner designers. Returning in 1948, Shoup was not again under contract to Warners but he worked there so steadily during the following twenty years that he only had time for three outside films. He did many of the big glamour pictures of the 1950s such as *Young in Heart* (1954) with Doris Day, and *Serenade* (1956) with Joan Fontaine and Mario Lanza.

The late fifties brought a new emphasis on youth to Warner Brothers and Shoup immediately adjusted to this. 'Natalie Wood and Suzanne Pleshette

on page 92
Leah Rhodes, Hedy Lamarr and Hal
Wallis discuss designs for *The
Conspirators* (1945).

on page 93
Cecil Beaton: Audrey Hepburn in her
Ascot hat in *My Fair Lady* (1964).

Howard Shoup: Doris Day in a costume test for *Young in Heart* (1954).

didn't care whether it was becoming or not, they wanted it right. I practically fainted one day when Natalie said "I think this should be aged." ' *Hotel* (1967) was the last film Shoup designed (although Edith Head dressed Merle Oberon), before retiring. He has only worked on two films since then. At the request of an old friend, Ray Stark, who knew he had worked for Ziegfield, Shoup helped with *Funny Girl* (1968) although Barbra Streisand was costumed by Irene Sharaff. Then Suzanne Pleshette asked him to do her clothes for *If It's Sunday, This Must be Belguim* (1969).

Since Shoup's departure, all Warners designers have been contracted one film at a time. Recent important costume assignments at Warners have included John Truscott's *Camelot* (1968) and Theodora Van Runkle's *Bonnie and Clyde* (1967) and *Mame* (1974).

94

Fox Finesse

on previous page
Royer: Loretta Young in the huge hoopskirts in *Suez* (1938).

René Hubert: Gloria Swanson in *Music in the Air* (1934), wearing a black crepe dress with Hubert's characteristic slit in the skirt.

Fox was one of Hollywood's oldest studios; it originated in 1914, yet it was not until the arrival of Darryl Zanuck in 1935 that the various production departments, including the wardrobe, became well organized, and it was almost another ten years before Charles LeMaire arrived and gave the Fox ladies a really definitive look. Most Fox designers had one trait in common: their tenures were never long. Thus Fox was never identified with a particular designer in the way MGM was associated with Adrian, and Paramount with Head.

Sophie Wachner, who came from MGM, was the first person to operate a cohesive wardrobe in the mid-1920s. But while she was there, Fox brought in outside designers for special films. Adrian, Kathleen Kay, Edward Stevenson, Dolly Tree, David Cox and Russell Patterson all came for short periods. After Wachner left, the succession of designers continued. Earl Luick came to do some of Fox's most prestigious films, including *Cavalcade* (1935). He was followed by Rita Kaufman, an elegant society lady married to a producer. She relied on sketch artists to do the actual designing and bought whole collections from Hattie Carnegie which she copied for the films, but she put it all together in a highly satisfactory manner. Helen Rose, whose career began as one of Kaufman's sketchers, remembers, 'She had two or three of us kids and we'd sit in a room. She'd come in and say, "Give me a black chiffon" or "we need an 1890s dress" and we'd draw some ideas. We never knew what picture they were for.'

Royer, who specialized in foreign and dual language films, was given a seven year contract in 1933, but the wardrobe department remained disorganized and the parade of designers continued to pass through it. René Hubert came with Gloria Swanson in 1934 to do *Music in the Air* and stayed to do fifteen films in nine months. William Lambert and Charles LeMaire also both came for a short period in 1934. But in the same year Fox took a new lease of life when it merged with 20th Century Productions.

20th Century Productions had been organized by Joseph Schenck and Darryl F. Zanuck in 1932. It had used the Goldwyn wardrobe department and the Goldwyn designer, Omar Kiam, as much as possible. Kiam had designed lavish costume epics like *Cardinal Richelieu* (1934) and *Folies Bergères* (1935), which was Merle Oberon's first American film. Her face was highly lacquered and exotic looking, and Kiam capitalized on her voluptuous figure by keeping her as much as possible in low-cut evening gowns and negligées of shiny fabrics. When Kiam was not available, Zanuck hired Gwen Wakeling, a talented free-lance designer. In 1934 she had done *The House of Rothschild*, one of the most coveted design assignments of the year. It contained beautiful Empire gowns, many gracefully worn by a very blonde Loretta Young, all kinds of uniforms, and traditional Jewish clothes. The final sequence was in the newly introduced three-strip Technicolor, still very crude, but a vast improvement on the earlier two-colour process. The colours of the dyes were still blue, yellow and a brownish-red, rather than the cyan, yellow and magenta which were introduced in 1936.

As part of the merger, Zanuck made Arthur Levy general manager of the new 20th Century Fox wardrobe. Some of the Fox designers left, but Royer stayed on and Levy put Gwen Wakeling under contract. Together they formed a

Omar Kiam: Merle Oberon in *Folies Bergeres* (1935).

Gwen Wakeling: Florence Arliss, George Arliss, Loretta Young, Robert Young and C. Aubrey Smith in *The House of Rothschild* (1934).

highly productive department. They worked separately on their own films but were good friends. They both did modern fashions and period costumes equally well, so that Levy could assign any picture to either of them, although Royer usually handled the big costume epics. He remembers, 'It seems Darryl Zanuck became a historian and wanted to film every great person's life. He did a lot of them. I was always surprised he missed the popes.'

Although Zanuck was primarily interested in story values and had no interest in cultivating glamour queens like Crawford and Shearer, he did have one of Hollywood's most beautiful women in Loretta Young. Her proportions and posture were perfect, nothing had to be camouflaged. She was highly interested in her clothes and clever about them. Royer remembers affectionately, 'While Gwen or I worked on her screen wardrobes, she always ran in a few personal items that were made by Irene that she wanted the studio to pay for.' Young preferred soft, figure moulding drapery to the stiffer constructions that were becoming fashionable in the late 1930s. Wakeling cut her day dresses on the bias for pictures like *Ladies in Love* (1936) and made many evening gowns of chiffon or tulle. One of her designs for *Wife, Husband and Friend* (1939) had a beige satin underslip covered with varying thicknesses of black souffle. Royer says, 'Among

Royer

Gwen Wakeling: Loretta Young in *Wife, Husband and Friend* (1939), wearing a gown of black souffle over nude satin.

opposite
Omar Kiam: George Arliss in *Cardinal Richlieu* (1934).

all the rubbish, we had Loretta and that made life bearable.' She worked hard until she learned how to manage period clothes, turning her hoopskirts sideways to get through doors gracefully. She sailed around in the enormous *Suez* (1938) skirts beautifully. She practised sitting in her *Story of Alexander Graham Bell* (1939) bustles until she mastered the art and could carry the weight with ease. She always had a full length mirror placed right next to the camera and before each scene she checked her lighting and arranged the voluminous skirts and decorations to show the costume off most advantageously.

Wakeling and Royer both dressed Alice Faye, who was always totally agreeable about her clothes, although her figure was difficult because it was ahead of its time. Faye had the kind of proportions other Fox actresses twenty years later would struggle with bust pads, waist cinchers and girdles to achieve: a big bosom, small waist and flat derrière. Faye resented it when her plume and spangle type roles as well as her figure caused her to be compared to Mae West. To play down her bust in the modern dress films, Wakeling and Royer both frequently gave her dresses of black wool crepe which did not reflect light and was usually not used in films. Her curves at the sides were still evident, but the dull wool flattened her contours. Wakeling and Royer cut across her bosom with vertical and diagonal lines and put eye-catching detail at the neck or below the waist. They used puffed sleeves and ruffs of feathers or tulle as camouflage.

Royer designed Shirely Temple's clothes for *Baby Takes a Bow* (1935), but when Zanuck sold the highly popular designs to manufacturers, it was the Temples who received most of the money, as Shirley's mother had insisted on this arrangement as soon as she realized her daughter's impact on juvenile fashion.

Zanuck had produced lavishly at 20th Century Productions, but, faced with Fox's debts after the merger, he was forced to cut back quite considerably, and so was quick to get into the B picture market when theatres began showing double features in 1936. Herschel was asked to handle the B film designs, and since the unit was on a different lot, he had little contact with Royer and Wakeling. Herschel accumulated an impressive number of credits but many of his films required virtually no designing. Continuing characters in series like *Mr Moto* and *Charlie Chan* wore the same clothes in film after film, and stock was used as much as possible.

Even for the A films Fox designers were usually not allowed adequate budgets and had to be very adept at using stock wardrobe, Royer says, 'Zanuck was more interested in volume than in quality, even on the stars. The last two years I was there, we remade more old clothes than we made new.'

There were changes afoot, however, as the decade of the Depression was ending. The studio's financial position became much better and they began to use much more Technicolor. Late in 1939 Royer and Wakeling left to form a partnership and open a shop, and Travis Banton, the highly paid designer who had been with Paramount, was signed up instead. Wakeling then decided to return to Fox during 1941, although she did not stay long, because, as Wakeling complained, 'there were too many pictures and never enough time.' During his stay, Luick designed *Springtime in the Rockies* (1942). Cameraman Leon Shamroy was bored with Technicolor's tight restrictions on permissible shades and combinations of colours, so he asked Luick to dress Betty Grable in brighter colours and used sharper contrasts of colour between costumes and sets. Everybody was pleased with the result and it signalled the era of the super-garish Fox musicals of the 1940s.

Neither did Travis Banton stay with Fox for long. During his two-year con-

Travis Banton: Alice Faye in a very Poiret look for *Tin Pan Alley* (1941).

tract, he was assigned most of the colour films. He also made Alice Faye into a stunning *Lillian Russell* in 1940. For once the period costumes allowed her hour-glass figure to be emphasized rather than disguised, especially since the Hayes Office was briefly allowing some display of cleavage, providing the décolleté was true to the period. Banton always had a special affinity for the hour-glass figure and the bustle: as early as 1929 he had constructed beautiful bustles on Fay Wray for *Four Feathers* and following *Lillian Russell* he was to do the same for Kay Francis, Anne Baxter and Arlene Whelan in *Charley's Aunt* (1941).

Banton designed for Faye again in *That Night in Rio* (1941). He gave her a voluptuous evening gown of draped gold lamé and masses of jewels. It was one of his most beautiful creations, and suited her figure perfectly, but was not Faye's image of herself. So when Wakeling returned to Fox while Banton was working on Faye's costumes for her next film, *Weekend in Havanna* (1941), Faye made the studio reassign her wardrobe to her. As a result the gowns were not as stunning as Banton's, but Faye felt comfortable wearing them and they adroitly concealed the fact that she was pregnant.

opposite
Gwen Wakeling: Alice Faye in *Weekend in Havanna* (1941). The careful placing of the beading diverts the eye from Faye's pregnancy, without drawing undue attention to her bosom.

Royer: Alice Faye in *Rose of Washington Square* (1939). The blatant use of black and white was done for a purpose. Faye played an entertainer, and wore this while performing on stage, but during the rest of the film she wore her usual soft styles.

opposite
Travis Banton: the direct contrast in costume between Rita Hayworth and Linda Darnell in *Blood and Sand* (1941).

Yvonne Wood: Carmen Miranda and Alice Faye in *The Gang's All Here* (1943). Wartime shortages made it impossible to get enough matching shoes for all the chorus girls. Because Faye was pregnant, all the outfits had to be black and simple.

Banton's best job at Fox was *Blood and Sand* (1941), with Rita Hayworth's tightly draped white dress in the seduction scene and her hot pink one in the tango scene contrasting with Linda Darnell's innocent blues and traditional Spanish shapes.

In 1943 the wardrobe department was again reduced to shambles when Arthur Levy quit Fox, leaving no general manager, and only one designer. Help arrived in the form of Charles LeMaire, a top Broadway designer who had just done a stint in the Army and was good at organizing people. All studio wardrobe departments had general managers, but LeMaire was the only one who supervised the designing as well as the sewing and indeed designed many films himself. After putting the sewing rooms in order, LeMaire assembled a staff of designers.

He assigned Yvonne Wood to musicals like *Sweet and Lowdown* and *Something For the Boys* (both 1944). Although Wood was most adept at the delightful nonsense of Carmen Miranda's hats, her talent for designing very masculine men's costumes brought her many assignments of realistic westerns later on. While at Fox she also covered up Alice Faye's second pregnancy in *The Gang's All Here* (1943) with a long, full skirt and with a strategically placed big, flat handbag.

opposite
Charles LeMaire: Betty Grable in *Billy Rose's Diamond Horseshoe* (1945).

Wood shared two films with Kay Nelson, who then did *Leave Her to Heaven* (1945), a Technicolor film in which the symbolic values of the clothes were very improtant. In the climactic scene when Tierney hurls herself down a flight of stairs to cause a miscarriage, Nelson dressed her in an aqua negligée to show her coldly calculating nature.

LeMaire brought in Bonnie Cashin for *The Keys of the Kingdom* (1943) and *Laura* (1944). *Laura* was just another black and white modern dress picture that nobody at the studio was very excited about, but Cashin made Gene Tierney's sudden appearance in the middle of the film very striking by putting her in a sudden revival of the cloche hat. Similar to the styles of 1929–30, it had a very wide brim which hung down to her collar at the back, covering her hair, while in the front, the brim was folded back over the crown to reveal Tierney's patrician brow. Its downward lines were sullen and provocative and when Laura appeared wearing it, the audience thought she was something special. Cashin was also very interested in ethnic clothing so LeMaire assigned her to *Anna and the King of Siam* (1946).

Although he preferred administrative work, LeMaire was sometimes prevailed upon to design as well. When Perlberg was producing *Billy Rose's Diamond Horseshoe* (1945), he insisted that LeMaire design the film since he had so often

Bonnie Cashin: Gene Tierney in the dramatic cloche hat in *Laura* (1944).

worked for Rose at the real Horseshoe in New York. LeMaire did not have time for the whole film, but he did the opening and closing numbers. George Seaton, the director, brought Margaret Dumont in to play a tiny bit part and remembers that LeMaire 'treated her like an empress. He even made sketches of the dresses he had in stock so she would think he was designing something just for her.'

LeMaire had problems with Betty Grable who became difficult and lost interest in her career after her marriage and the birth of her daughters. She refused to work with any of the Fox contract designers on *The Dolly Sisters* (1945), but fortunately LeMaire was suddenly asked to give Orry Kelly a job by Joseph Schenck. The Technicolor absurdity of a Betty Grable picture was as far

Orry Kelly: Betty Grable and June Haver in *The Dolly Sisters* (1945).

removed from the grim black and white reality of the standard Warner fare as anything could possibly be, but Kelly loved the assignment and constructed the spangles and plumes for Grable and June Haver brilliantly. However, he did not work so well with Betty Grable on *The Shocking Miss Pilgrim* (1947) when he had to try and tone down her brassy image, and during their next collaboration, *Mother Wore Tights* (1947) Grable had her own way throughout. Although the film was set in 1900–20, Grable insisted on showing as much of her legs as possible, wearing pastel pumps, nude hose and mid-calf skirts with slits, often looking completely contemporary except for her slightly lower hems. After that Kelly could not work with her.

Rene Hubert also came back to Fox. Hubert had previously designed for Fox in London for several years, and was delighted to be assigned *Wilson* (1944). It was set in America during the First World War, so costumes were elegant, there were no powerful women stars to force him to modernize the styles – indeed even Zanuck insisted that every detail should be correct, and the budget was unlimited.

René Hubert inherited Grable for *That Lady in Ermine* (1948), but fortunately the period of the 1860s called for uncompromising hoop-skirts and the plot contained enough opportunities for Grable to display her legs to satisfy her. The dream sequence had her dancing with Douglas Fairbanks Jr in an enormous hoopskirt of transparent white chiffon which frequently flew up (see page 122).

Hubert was ranked with Walter Plunkett as the industry's most respected expert on period work, but he did as many modern dress films as period in his career. *State Fair* (1945) was in modern dress, though Hubert conceived it in fairytale terms. *Centennial Summer* (1946), set in 1876, demonstrates his period talent. Although the styles are copied faithfully, Hubert 'made the colours brighter and used lighter weight materials because', he explained, 'the actresses couldn't walk naturally in such heavy dresses.' Again in *The Foxes of Harrow* (1947) Hubert cleverly adapted Rex Harrison's tailcoat and gave him light trousers to make him look heavier, while he cut Richard Haydn's coat tails to cover his sides and slim him down.

Hubert was one of the few to come off with any distinction in *Forever Amber* (1947). LeMaire gave him the assignment before the title role had been cast, and so great was his enthusiasm that Hubert made many sketches for the voluptuous Amber of the novel. But none of them were useable, because Zanuck gave the role to Peggy Cummins, who was little and wiry. Shooting started but then stopped, and Zanuck announced that Linda Darnell would take over as Amber, so Hubert returned to his original sketches (see page 119). His best dress for her was a black and white striped satin, cut to slim her and trimmed with many red ribbons. Hubert returned to Europe in 1949, but before he left he worked with Marilyn Monroe on *Ticket to Tomahawk* (1949).

At the request of Bette Davis, Head came in to design her wardrobe for *All About Eve* (1950). LeMaire supervised and designed the rest of the cast's clothes. The film is a classic example of how unremarkable clothes can subconsciously strengthen the characterizations in the mind of the viewer. Together Head and LeMaire decided that Anne Baxter's Eve would be a drab little wren until the party scene, when, wearing one of Margo's cast-off dresses, her behaviour begins to betray her ploy.

As usual, Bette Davis had a lot of ideas about how she should dress for Margo: stylish but a little overdone. When Head suggested that Davis should wear mostly full skirts, but a tight one in the theatre where Margo insults all her friends and ends up alone, Davis suddenly ran across Head's office and flung

René Hubert: Constance Bennett in *Centennial Summer* (1946).

René Hubert: Marilyn Monroe in a
costume test for *Ticket to Tomahawk*
(1949), the first costume to be designed
for Monroe at Fox.

opposite
René Hubert: a sketch for Peggy Cummins
in *Forever Amber* (1947).

on page 114
top left
Mitchell Leisen: a costume for Douglas
Fairbanks in *The Thief of Bagdad* (1923,
United Artists).

top right
Edward Stevenson: a costume sketch for
Norma Talmadge in *The Lady* (1924, First
National).

bottom left
Howard Greer: a costume sketch for
Kathlyn Williams in *The Spanish
Dancer* (1923, Famous Players-Lasky).

bottom right
Natacha Rambova: a costume sketch for
De Mille's *Saturday Night* (1922, Famous
Players-Lasky).

on page 115
Travis Banton: Claudette Colbert in
Cleopatra (1934, Paramount), dressed in
an adaption of the famous Colbert Collar.

Amber

Rene Hubert

front with bow tie
white tie silk
blouse
out
Handkerchiefs - Out
Diamond pins
pumps
bl. kid
Out
MANKIEWICZ - A597
BETTE DAVIS
AS "MARGO"
CH# 9
EXT. N.Y. THEATRE
81
INT. LOBBY & FOYER
82
INT. THEATRE 83
4/2/50 DES-HEAD

herself on the divan. That business was not in the script, but she had already decided how she would play the scene and said, 'make the skirt full enough for me to do that'. When the suit was made and tested, Davis asked Head for a different blouse, one with frills at the neck, because she envisioned that Margo's final insults would be shot in such a tight close-up that only her neck would show and she wanted something to indicate her feminity.*

Davis' now well-known dress for the party scene was a happy accident. Made up the night before it was needed, there was no time for a fitting. Head was horrified when Davis put it on. It was too big and the top slid off her shoulders. Davis laughed and said she liked it better that way! Head and LeMaire shared the Oscar for Best Black and White Design for the film in 1951.

LeMaire was fortunate that RKO shut down at the same time as Hubert left and he was able to hire Edward Stevenson to concentrate on period and character clothes to replace him as far as possible. Stevenson did three films set at the turn and early in this century, but his best assignment at Fox was the biblical epic *David and Bathsheba* (1952). He worked on it for months with an archaeologist and was rewarded with an Oscar nomination for the Best Colour Costume

on page 118
Dorothy Lamour in a sarong. The first of these famous costumes was designed by Edith Head for Lamour in *Jungle Princess* (1936, Paramount) and started a vogue for tropical fabrics and sarong draping that lasted throughout the second world war.

on page 119
René Hubert: Linda Darnell in *Forever Amber* (1947, Fox).

Edith Head: Bette Davis in *All About Eve* (1950):
opposite a costume test
below how the costume finally appeared on the screen.

* Actually, director Joseph Mankiewicz used a somewhat longer shot.

opposite
William Travilla: Betty Grable in the
'Heat Wave in Alaska' number from
Meet Me after the Show (1951).

Design in 1952. Unfortunately he had to leave in 1953 to undergo cataract operations in both eyes.

LeMaire hired new designers again when Yvonne Wood and Bonnie Cashin left. He was pleased when Renie, a colleague of Stevenson's at RKO, accepted his invitation to join Fox, because, as he says, 'She can do any kind of picture well'.

LeMaire was also pleased when William Travilla came to Fox because, 'Right from the start everything he did was good'.

LeMaire assigned Travilla to mostly male pictures because of his success with Errol Flynn at Warners. Then he was assigned Betty Grable in *Meet Me After the Show* (1951). For the 'Heat Wave in Alaska' number Travilla dressed her in a strapless black bathing suit trimmed with ermine tails and ear muffs! 'From then on, I was stuck with the sex symbols,' he said.

Edward Stevenson: Gregory Peck in
David and Bathsheba (1951).

on page 122
René Hubert: Betty Grable and Douglas
Fairbanks Jnr in the dream sequence
from *That Lady in Ermine* (1948, Fox).

on page 123
Edith Head and Dorothy Jeakins: Hedy
Lamarr and Victor Mature in *Samson and
Delilah* (1949, Paramount).

On the chalkboard:
HAWKS A 698
MARILYN MONROE
AS "LORELEI"
CH #10
INT SHIPS CORRIDOR
44, 45
INT MALONES CABIN 4697
ON BOAT DECK-48
ON TELEPHONE-50
CH #11
INT LORELEIS LIVING
ROOM-52,54, 55
INT BEDROOM-53
AT PORTHOLE-56
EXT DECK-57
DES-TRAVILLA
11/28/52

opposite
William Travilla: Marilyn Monroe in a
costume test for *River of No Return*
(1954), a dress constructed of green
velvet and wire and a bit of black lace to
mask her cleavage.

William Travilla helps Marilyn Monroe
with a costume test for *Gentlemen Prefer
Blondes* (1953).

Once Marilyn Monroe became a star, all her costumes were designed by
Travilla, 'Sex symbols can be difficult because they know their appeal is based on
just one thing and they have to keep that before the public at all times.'
Marilyn Monroe exploited her body and her walk constantly. She had crooked
legs and weak ankles and her buttocks naturally swayed from side to side when
she walked. When she saw the response it got, she exaggerated it and insisted on
tight skirts to play it up and her directors obligingly photographed her from the
back whenever they could. Only twice did she wear full skirts, in *Monkey Business* (1952) so she could stick her leg on the couch next to Cary Grant and pull
the skirt up to reveal her stocking, and in *The Seven Year Itch* (1955) so it could
blow up with the breeze from the subway.

Monroe knew her legs were not up to the Grable standard of beauty, but she
always managed to pose them advantageously even for the wardrobe department tests. Coping with her breasts was an engineering problem Travilla had to
solve with every costume. Monroe and Jane Russell could be photographed in

on page 126
top Irene Sharaff: Leslie Caron in *An
American in Paris* (1951, MGM).

bottom William Travilla: Marilyn Monroe,
Betty Grable and Lauren Bacall in *How
to Marry a Millionaire* (1953, Fox).

on page 127
top Charles LeMaire: Jean Simmons,
Ernest Thesiger and Richard Burton in
The Robe (1953, Fox), one of the first
films to use Cinemascope Technicolor.

bottom Orry Kelly: a scene from *Oklahoma!*
(1955, MGM), showing many of the
costumes he designed.

Irene Sharaff

public showing as much cleavage as they liked, but Fox was afraid to release any film or stills of them showing cleavage. Travilla also had to wire the inside of each dress to keep their breasts from bouncing when they walked or danced. The stars shook a lot in the 'Little Girl from Little Rock' number in *Gentlemen Prefer Blondes* (1953) but their bosoms did not budge. The costume Travilla originally designed for the 'Diamonds Are a Girl's Best Friend' scene was a further triumph in wires and souffle. Monroe was to become a giant necklace, seemingly nude except for bands of black velvet and masses of rhinestones. The costume cost over $5000 in materials and expert labour necessary to dye the souffle to match her flesh, construct an elaborate network of wires and apply the stones. It did not break any rules since there was no cleavage and the breasts were firmly anchored in place. But the notoriety of the calendar was by then so great that Fox was considering shutting down the film and Travilla was told to make another, 'absolutely sexless' costume for Monroe. He made it of shocking pink upholstery satin lined with felt to make it even stiffer, 'but on Monroe, it moved sensually anyway,' he remembers.

Despite the fame of his association with Monroe, Travilla preferred assignments for character clothes, like *Viva Zapata* (1952), when he 'enjoyed transforming Jean Peters, a pretty all-American girl into the simple Mexican peasant. To break up her big, confident stride, I asked her to wear shoes that were a half size too small. They were just uncomfortable enough to make her walk slower, almost cautiously. Jean was very long waisted and most Mexican women are short waisted, so I made a body pad which raised her hips. All her clothes were five years behind the date of the picture to show her poverty.'

Cinemascope, introduced with *The Robe* in 1953 (see page 127), while a financial bonanza for 20th Century Fox, was a headache for the designers. LeMaire designed *The Robe* when it was first conceived in black and white. When the studio decided to switch to colour, many costumes had to be bleached out and re-dyed and others replaced. Then the film was postponed again until tests were made to determine how to deal with Cinemascope. LeMaire noticed that despite the graininess and the distortions, the magnification was now so much greater that detail became terribly important. Machine stitching that had never showed now had to be pulled out and redone by hand.

Travilla, who designed the second 'Scope film, *How to Marry a Millionaire* (1953) remembers, 'Zanuck, the labs, everybody kept insisting there were no distortions with 'Scope. In truth there were such terrible distortions they couldn't shoot close-ups at all, and everybody was definitely widened.' Although the prevailing style of enormously full skirts made waistlines seem smaller, all three stars, Marilyn Monroe, Betty Grable and Lauren Bacall refused to wear them; each wanted the slimmest possible skirts. LeMaire did not want Fox designers to appear ignorant of current fashion, so he called a meeting. Grable finally agreed to wear a cancan petticoat under a very full blue taffeta dress in the first scenes; Bacall wore a full-skirted printed shirtwaist in the fashion show and a couple of her others flared; but Monroe was completely intransigent and insisted on tight skirts (see page 126).

The credits on every Fox film read, 'Costume supervision by Charles LeMaire, Costumes designed by . . .'. Aside from the films he designed himself, LeMaire's participation on the others varied depending on the designer. Usually he checked over all the sketches, was present at the fittings and supervised on days when there were crowds of extras. Irene Dunne remembers LeMaire at her fittings for *Anna and the King of Siam*, 'It was a very long schedule, with many costume changes, and it was hard to find time to fit them in. But never in my life have I done a picture where everything fitted so perfectly the very first time I tried them on. Irene ran a tight ship over at MGM but LeMaire's supervision was even tighter.' Some designers resented this and when *The Model and the Marriage Broker* was nominated for Best Black and White Design in 1952, Renie was under a lot of pressure from certain colleagues to take LeMaire's name off the nomination. 'But', she says, 'he gave me the job in the first place and he always stood behind his designers all the way. He would have defended us to Zanuck if he had to.'

LeMaire was not credited on every film, however. Irene Sharaff, brought in from New York for *Call Me Madam* (1953), absolutely refused to let LeMaire have any screen credit and did the whole film without consulting him. It was a beautiful job. Ethel Merman, introduced as the snappy, tight-skirted and tailored ambassadress to Lichtenstein, gradually let her clothes take on a softer, peasant flavour.

Having designed the stage version of *The King and I*, Sharaff returned to Fox for the film in 1956. Deborah Kerr says, 'Irene Sharaff is a brilliant woman. I did think, however, that those hoopskirts were terribly big and that the engravings of the period exaggerated their size the way our fashion illustrations today elongate the figure. But she insisted that she had some actual measurements of hoops. The hoops were made of metal and were extremely heavy, but that gave the skirts a flow they wouldn't have had if they had been cane. I had to put foam rubber pads on my hips in the "Shall We Dance" number to keep from injuring myself with the hoops.' Sharaff also came to design Elizabeth Taylor's splendid robes for the massive *Cleopatra* (1963). Renie dressed the supporting women and Vittoria Nino Novarese dressed all the men. All three won the Oscar for Best Colour Design in 1964.

Susan Hayward was the most loyal of the stars that LeMaire designed for personally. He understood her well and assigned himself to most of the films she did at 20th Century Fox. Of Hayward's well-known temperament, LeMaire says, 'Susie was first and foremost a wife and mother and when things weren't going well at home, she'd get edgy at the studio', but she entered into her role as the crippled singer Jane Froman in *With a Song in My Heart* (1952) with passionate intensity. Jane Froman spent a week with LeMaire, describing the kind of clothes she had worn before and after her accident. Although LeMaire made no exact duplicates, everything was correct for the period. Froman taught Hayward how she sang, and although it was Froman's voice on the tracks, Hayward belted the songs out when she filmed the numbers. This so impressed LeMaire that he made the waistlines of the dresses tight and clinging so the expansion and contraction of her stomach muscles would show.

Dorothy Jeakins, who had been a sketch artist at Fox in 1938, returned for three years in the early 1950s. She had a particularly good eye for colour, 'You give Dorothy a piece of cloth and she will strip it, re-dye it and over-dye it until she gets just the colour she has in mind,' says Head, who worked with her on De Mille epics at Paramount. She specialized in ethnic and period assignments, and she designed *Niagra* (1953) which included the famous magenta dress in which Marilyn Monroe sang 'Kiss me'. She came back again for *South Pacific* (1958) and *Sound of Music* (1965) (both of which she had earlier created on Broadway), was requested by Marilyn Monroe for *Let's Make Love* (1960) and Mel Brooks for *Young Frankenstein* (1974).

Desirée (1954) brought René Hubert back to Fox at the request of Merle Oberon. He received Oscar nominations for it as well as his last two Fox pictures, both filmed in Europe, *Anastasia* (1956) and *The Visit* (1961). He says of the star

on pages 130 and 131
Irene Sharaff: a scene from *The King and I* (1956) with Deborah Kerr in the mammoth hoopskirts.

Ingrid Bergman, 'A most charming star, great in her simplicity and naturalness. For the nominations, I have to thank her for her elegance in wearing my gowns.' Hubert has refused all film offers since but remains active in the theatre in Europe.

There were other Fox designers during this period, including Mary Wills, Adele Palmer, Adele Balkan and Elois Jenssen. Now that he had fewer films to supervise LeMaire could undertake more design himself. However, after Darryl Zanuck left in 1957 and Buddy Adler bedame head of the studio, the budget for sets and costumes was reduced, curtailing LeMaire's ideas. When his contract expired in 1959 he left, but returned for Susan Hayward's *Marriage-Go-Round* in 1960 and Jennifer Jones' *Tender is the Night* in 1962. LeMaire's first project with Jones, *Love is a Many-Splendored Thing* (1955) had won him an Oscar, and though *Tender's* designer was Pierre Balmain, LeMaire stepped in for refittings and other work as a favour to Jones.

After LeMaire's departure, there were few pictures calling for the kind of enormous wardrobes his department had once routinely provided. Fox's last

opposite
Charles LeMaire: Susan Hayward portrays Jane Froman in *With a Song in My Heart* (1952).

Charles LeMaire: a scene from *Love is a Many Splendored Thing* (1955), with Jennifer Jones, which started a trend towards oriental fashion.

Helen Rose: Debbie Reynolds in *Goodbye Charlie* (1966), wearing an evening gown completely embroidered in white and crystal beads. This was one of the last times a woman in a modern dress film was glamourized for the sake of it.

great epic, *Cleopatra* (1963), lost money for the studio. Despite excellent costuming, the studio's last two big musicals, *Star* (designed by Donald Brooks, 1968), and *Hello Dolly* (designed by Irene Sharaff, 1969), shared the same fate. The company's most recent blockbuster, *The Towering Inferno* (1974) did, however, show a significant return to high fashion elegance in Paul Zastupnevich's designs.

RKO Ingenuity

on previous page
Walter Plunkett and his assistant
construct a costume for chorus girl, Anna
Karina, for a forgotten musical of 1929.

During its thirty year span of existence, RKO made many noteworthy films, but the nearly constant state of bankruptcy in which the studio had to operate, and the scarcity of glamorous stars, meant that the designers' work usually had to be realistic rather than opulent.

The RKO wardrobe department and Walter Plunkett's career as a designer began simultaneously in 1926, though RKO was a small studio then known as FBO. At first Plunkett just rented clothes and made budget estimations. FBO made many two-reel comedies about policemen or secretaries, and Plunkett realized that in the long run buying uniforms was less expensive than renting them, and that making frocks was cheaper than buying them. So he hired seamstresses and set up a workroom. FBO also made a lot of westerns and because the wild shirts and pants needed could not be purchased, Plunkett had to begin to make those too. As a result, unlike most designers, he learned about male clothes as well as female. Plunkett had no formal training and had to learn by observation and practical experience, but soon his department was making everything the studio needed.

Talking pictures brought a series of mergers, the studio was renamed RKO and William LeBaron became the head of production. LeBaron instituted productions like *Rio Rita* (1929) which were far more lavish than anything Plunkett had ever worked on before. *Rio Rita* introduced Plunkett to two-colour Technicolor and he made Bebe Daniels a dress that was watermelon pink trimmed in turquoise, the two colours which would reproduce. 'Also Bebe was always anxious to have lots of rhinestones and cloth of gold so I made a dress that was cloth of gold from the top of her mantilla to her feet. I saw the picture recently and it was hysterical, but at the time, we thought it was beautiful. The camera didn't get the actual colour of it, but it had the metallic quality.'

Cimarron (1931) was Plunkett's first big costume picture. The star, Irene Dunne and the director, Wesley Ruggles, were both sceptical when Plunkett showed them a sketch with the big 1890s leg-o-mutton sleeves. They knew that audiences were not used to seeing anything as extreme as that, yet they wanted the film to be correct. Eventually the sleeves featured in the dialogue. At the first reaction to them in the film Dunne says, 'They say in Chicago that they'll be even bigger by fall'.

Although Dunne was a fine actress, she was initially rather stocky and awkward in her movements, but by the time Plunkett put her in period costumes again for *Stingaree* (1934) and *Age of Innocence* (1935) she had slimmed down and learned to carry the heavy dresses gracefully.

In 1931 RKO and Pathe merged and Gwen Wakeling who had worked for Pathe came to RKO to finish the pictures she had already started, but did not stay on after that. Ann Harding, who had been dressed by Wakeling at Pathe, was dressed by Plunkett at RKO. She starred in *The Life of Vergie Winters* (1934) as a long suffering milliner. As well as the dresses, Plunkett designed dozens of hats which were used as props, the changing styles indicating the passage of time. With her naturally pale blonde hair that fell to her waist, Harding was very beautiful. While most actresses need at least a white collar around the neck to reflect light up and soften the lines of their faces, Plunkett usually tried to put black or other dark colours around Harding's face to give her finely chiselled features more definition.

For a short while in 1932, after a dispute with the management of RKO, Plunkett worked for Western Costume and Harding was dressed by Irene for *The Animal Kingdom* (1932). Dolores del Rio asked Irene to do her costumes for *Flying Down to Rio* (1933), but Plunkett, who had returned, designed for Fred Astaire and Ginger Rogers. In 1934 Plunkett dressed Rogers again for *The Gay Divorcee* and remembers, 'Ginger wanted more ornate stuff, Fred wanted simple things that moved just right, and the director, Mark Sandrich, with his eye to the camera, had strong ideas. Some of the sketches I had to revise five or six times before I got one they all agreed on. And Ginger, you always had to slip into her dressing room just before she shot the first scene in a new dress to make sure she didn't stick a flower in her hair and add more jewellery.'

Although Katharine Hepburn's debut film, *A Bill of Divorcement* (1932) was designed by Josette de Lima during Plunkett's absence from RKO, he worked on three films with her in 1933 including *Little Women* when he proved a match for

Walter Plunkett: a scene from *Rio Rita* (1929) with Bebe Daniels.

the Hepburn spirit. Hepburn came for a preliminary meeting and borrowed a hoopskirt to practise her walk, but after one fitting, did not come in again. Shooting started with only two dresses finished. When the assistant director expressed concern Hepburn snapped, 'So what?' Plunkett, usually mild mannered, retaliated, 'From the way you are starting, you'll soon be a worse bitch than Constance Bennett.' Hepburn thought this was hysterically funny and laughed, 'Darling, I'll be up at noon every day. I don't need lunch. We'll get everything fitted!'

Plunkett emphasized the poverty in *Little Women* in several ways. He made the sisters exchange their clothes, and used cheap calicos and rough knitted shawls and mittens. Another problem for him was to make the twenty-two year old Joan Bennett into a convincing ten year old, which was made more difficult when he learned that Bennett was pregnant.

By 1935, Plunkett's position at RKO was highly unsatisfactory. 'I was not only the designer but manager of the wardrobe department. I had the payroll, the hiring and firing of seamstresses and the budget to look after as well as

opposite
Walter Plunkett: Irene Dunne in *Age of Innocence* (1934), wearing a stylized turn-of-the-century frock.

Walter Plunkett: Frances Dee, Katharine Hepburn, Jean Parker and Joan Bennett in *Little Women* (1933).

making my own sketches and the clothes. I had no contract, no screen credit half the time, was earning $75 a week, they were giving the best pictures to Bernard Newman.' So saying, Plunkett went off to New York and the wholesale business.

Bernard Newman, a high class couturier had come to RKO from New York in 1934. Irene Dunne knew Newman and had recommended him to the studio when it started planning the high-fashion *Roberta* (1935). Although RKO did not need and could not afford another full-time designer, it contracted Newman with great fanfare, and told the press he had spent $250,000 on the costumes. Whatever they cost, the fashions were stupendous. The show at the end revealed Newman's fascination with the wet look: Ginger Rogers wore a fantastic wet seal gown of black slipper satin that fitted her like a coat of paint. Ironically, Irene Dunne did not fare so well. Drapes of white satin crossed over her chest to make it look fuller only succeeded in making her back looked hunched, though Newman did give her an attractive tight little wig, pomaded heavily for his favoured wet look.

Newman continued at RKO through 1935 and 1936, designing many films including two more with Astaire and Rogers. He understood the needs of their dances better than their other designers. For pure grace of line and movement, the gown for the erotic 'Let's Face the Music and Dance' number in *Follow the Fleet* (1936) was the most beautiful of all. It was pale grey chiffon covered with crystal beads. The weight of the skirt when motionless made it cling tightly to Rogers' body, but when she danced, it opened like a flower. Expert lighting made it transparent, showing her beautiful legs. Unfortunately the sleeves, constructed the same way, hit Astaire's face with stunning force and the skirt battered both partners' legs, but the result on film was sublime.

After Plunkett left, Newman had to do the routine RKO assignments to which he was wholly unsuited. Edward Stevenson, who became Newman's sketch artist, explained, 'Newman draped material on the actress until he got an idea. The stars got exhausted and the studio couldn't spare them for the time it took. When he thought he had it, I would make the sketch, but he kept changing those too.' Newman could not churn out designs fast enough, nor could he reconcile himself to figures less perfect than that of Ginger Rogers. He finally quit RKO, recommending that Stevenson replace him.

Edward Stevenson had been in the business a dozen years when he became head designer at RKO, which was now, more than ever, a poor studio. He did not try to follow Newman's example. 'I didn't have the scripts or the stars for such fabulous clothes. I always tried to design clothes that supported the script and didn't detract from it.' Lucille Ball, whose loyalty to Stevenson was lifelong, says of their early days at RKO, 'He didn't try to please everybody. He read the script and he understood the character I was playing and he stuck to his guns when somebody wanted to change it. I made those B pictures so fast, we were usually working on two or three wardrobes at once. Poor as RKO was in most respects, they always made clothes for me rather than buy them.'

One of Stevenson's few lavish assignments was Lily Pons' *That Girl from Paris* (1936) which was complicated by the fact that Pons was being courted by Andre Kostalanetz, who sent her an orchid every day which she wanted to stick on her costume even though it was often inappropriate. But in general RKO's limited number of glamorous assignments eluded Stevenson. Katharine Hepburn insisted that Plunkett be brought back from New York for *Mary of Scotland* (1936) and all her period films; she used Muriel King for *Stage Door* (1937) and Howard Greer for *Bringing up Baby* (1938).

opposite
Bernard Newman: Lucille Ball as one of
the mannequins in *Roberta*'s climactic
fashion show.

Bernard Newman: Ginger Rogers in the
'Let's Face the Music and Dance'
number from *Follow the Fleet* (1936).

Plunkett had returned to Hollywood in 1936 to specialize in period costumes, and, working freelance, he was asked to design several films for RKO including *The Story of Vernon and Irene Castle* (1939) with Ginger Rogers. Irene Castle, the popular dancer, had been a fashion innovator in the first world war era, and Plunkett followed her actual clothes as closely as possible, adapting them to Rogers' movements and the needs of the camera. Suddenly Mrs Castle arrived and reminded RKO that in exchange for the film rights they had guaranteed her the right to design Rogers' wardrobe. The studio compromised by agreeing that she and Rogers could have a fitting on each dress without Plunkett present. To get around this, Plunkett and Rogers had secret meetings, and then at the fitting, Rogers would suggest to Mrs Castle all the things she and Plunkett had decided upon. Then Rogers wanted her hair at its usual shoulder length, instead of in the Castle bob. She refused to cut it or wear a wig. Finally she compromised by curling it up as tightly as possible. In the end, Mrs Castle was credited for Rogers' clothes, and Plunkett for the rest.

Walter Plunkett: Ginger Rogers and Fred Astaire in *The Story of Vernon and Irene Castle* (1939).

opposite
Walter Plunkett: Katharine Hepburn in *Mary of Scotland* (1935).

145

Ginger Rogers in a test of the compromise version of the Irene Castle bob. Even curled up this tightly, Rogers' hair was considerably longer than Irene Castle's had been.

Renie working with Ginger Rogers on *Tom, Dick and Harry* (1941).

opposite
Irene: Ginger Rogers in *Lucky Partners* (1941); full skirts were gradually returning when wartime shortages put an end to them. (The Hayes Office refused to let this still be published because the posing of the legs was thought too suggestive.)

During the next few years Rogers worked with several designers, but most frequently with Renie, who had originally been hired in 1937 to do the RKO B pictures. She had designed many wild numbers for Lupe Velez' *Mexican Spitfire* series and Wendy Barrie's *Saint* and *Falcon* series, and had also done some A assignments. She had been friendly with Ginger Rogers for years and when Rogers decided to dye her hair brown and tone down both her brassiness and her glamour she enlisted Renie. 'Ginger could be mighty difficult and very sweet, all at the same time. *Tom, Dick and Harry* (1941) had so many clothes that they weren't all made when we started shooting, and the only time we could fit was every night after shooting. She was exhausted and would complain, but usually she was concerned about the good of the picture. I'd rather have that than somebody who just doesn't care.'

Rogers continued to want to work with different designers. She decided to use Irene for *Lucky Partners* (1940), Edith Head for *Tender Comrade* (1943) and Leslie Morris for *Once Upon a Honeymoon* (1943).

RKO's lesser leading ladies continued to be dressed by Edward Stevenson. He had costumed Joan Fontaine for several films and was pleased to see her return for *Suspicion* (1941), now a big star after *Rebecca* (1940). Her figure, always slender, was now reed thin and Stevenson was delighted to be able to forget slimming tricks and give Fontaine suits with straight-as-arrow skirts and a nightgown full of fattening tucks and pleats for her fatal glass of milk scene.

Orson Welles asked Stevenson to do two films. *Citizen Kane* (1941) was an exciting assignment as Welles wanted accurate period clothes and the women were actresses rather than the usual movie stars with notions of what they would and would not wear. Stevenson assumed that it was common knowledge that the film was about William Randolph Hearst and Marion Davies, especially since

Welles supplied him with dozens of stills of Marion Davies to use as research in designing Dorothy Commingore's costumes, and was always amused when Welles denied it later.

Filming was well under way when Dorothy Commingore confessed she was pregnant. Welles managed to hide this by having her seated behind tables or lying down until the climactic scene in which she left Kane which had to be played standing up, full figure. Letting out the seams ruined the authenticity of her early 1930s outfit and when that did not completely hide the pregnancy, Stevenson gave Commingore an enormous muff to carry. It created a continuity problem since Kane and his wife were supposed to be in Florida in summer, but there was no other solution.

RKO made its first three-strip Technicolor film, *The Spanish Main* in 1945. Stevenson clearly enjoyed the new medium. The only costume problem concerned Maureen O'Hara and her bosom. Although her gowns were low-cut, Stevenson had checked that no cleavage showed. However, during filming, the front office angrily complained there was a definite space between her breasts. When Stevenson confronted O'Hara she admitted she had a method of dealing with the censors: she grasped the waistband and pulled down on it, at the same time taking a deep breath until her breasts almost popped out of the dress. Seeing how much trouble this would cause Stevenson, she agreed to behave.

Edward Stevenson: Anna Neagle tries on the celebrated Alice blue gown of *Irene* (1940).

opposite
Edward Stevenson: Dorothy Commingore in *Citizen Kane* (1941).

Michael Woulfe: Jane Russell in the gold mesh dress in *Macao* (1952).

Stevenson's last big assignment was to pad up the now very slender Irene Dunne into a buxom peasant in *I Remember Mama* (1948) while Gile Steel costumed the men. Stevenson remembers, 'Irene Dunne, whose facial features are patrician, was extremely difficult to transform into an earthy Norwegian mother. Exhaustive tests were made until the simplest effects were achieved.'

Howard Hughes assumed control of RKO in 1949 and shut the studio down. Renie had left in 1947 and Stevenson only stayed on the payroll for a few months until his contract expired when he went to Fox. When production resumed, the first film, *The Women on Pier 13*, starred Loraine Day who asked for Michael Woulfe to design her wardrobe. Woulfe had done two earlier RKO pictures for Day, and was eventually given a contract. However, Hughes' favourite designer had been Howard Greer since the days of Jean Harlow's *Hells Angels* (1930) and so he sent all his special protégés, such as Janet Leigh in *Holiday Affair* (1950), to Greer. But when Ava Gardner insisted on Woulfe for *My Forbidden Past* (1951), Hughes began to entrust him with all the RKO stars, even Jane Russell.

Unfortunately for Woulfe, most of the RKO scripts were trite and Hughes' concept of women was vulgar. Woulfe was ordered to accentuate Jane Russell's breasts and keep them on display at all times. Regardless of day or evening, appropriate to the plot or not, every change had the same low décolletage and every skirt had to be tight. For *Macao* (1952) Josef von Sternberg was determined to give Russell a new image and told Woulfe to keep her covered up. Hughes was furious when he saw the tests. and Woulfe had to design an entire new wardrobe. Only the famous gold mesh dress was retained. Woulfe later designed Russell's notorious dancing costume in *The French Line* (1954). Through much of the ensuing controversy and despite her religious activities, Jane Russell remained unperturbed. 'She looked at it as a job to do and her private life was another thing', says Woulfe, 'She was a great gal, but more of a tomboy at heart than anything else.'

Jane Russell's legs were so long she had a very short waistline. Woulfe used many tricks to elongate her waist including a wide black belt which had a greater diameter along the bottom so that it could be worn around her hips. He used the same idea on Jean Simmons, for she was also short-waisted, and once Judy Garland borrowed such a Woulfe-designed dress from Simmons. Garland asked Woulfe to design gowns for the three big premières of *A Star is Born*. Not only had she put on weight since the end of the film, she was also pregnant and wanted to keep it a secret. One design, now one of her best known costumes, was a fitted black velvet dress with a broad neckband of pink satin heavily beaded with crystal. He made a flat little pillbox hat of the satin which dripped crystal beads to 'draw the eye upward and make the costume start at the top of her head rather than the neckline', and she carried a black fox muff.

Hughes sold his RKO interests in 1955 and Woulfe joined his Howard Hughes Productions. The new owners kept up production for just over a year and employed freelance designers, including Edward Stevenson, who returned for Ginger Rogers' *The First Travelling Saleslady* (1956), and Renie, who did the very last RKO film, *The Girl Most Likely* (1958).

In 1958 Desilu Productions, half owned by Lucille Ball, bought the studio property. For Stevenson, the ten years designing *I Love Lucy* with Lucille Ball were heaven. Lucy's wild antics gave him a chance to design modest but pretty fashions, showgirl outfits and weird disguises. One of his favourite costumes was a deceptively simple-looking shirt that was lined with net so that Lucy could drop a dozen eggs inside and then dance a tango with Desi Arnaz.

opposite
Michael Woulfe: Jane Russell wearing the controversial costume for *The French Line* (1954); each of the tear-shaped holes was edged with wire and covered with nude souffle to prevent it buckling.

Renie: Simone Simon in *Curse of the Cat People* (1943). This excursion into vampire-horror design was very unusual for Renie, who normally did very conventional heroine frocks.

Stevenson's last film was *The Facts of Life* (1960) for which he shared an Oscar with Edith Head. Lucille Ball recalls, 'It was my first film in some time and I wanted Eddie (Stevenson), but the producers wanted Edith Head – who I enjoy working with too – so I didn't argue. Edith was very good about it, she said, "The workrooms at Paramount are busy so why don't you make the costumes up at Desilu and have Eddie supervise?" Eddie came to every fitting – he's a genius at tiny changes that make a big difference – and he bought all of the accessories. Edith made sure he got credit.' Despite his failing health and Lucille Ball's offer to retire him on full salary for life, Stevenson did not want to retire. Lucy's clothes grew more fashionable as the character became more affluent and in the later years, Stevenson also costumes such glamourous guests as Ethel Merman and Joan Crawford. He died while working in 1968. Soon Desilu was sold to Gulf and Western and the lot merged with adjoining Paramount. The RKO wardrobe was no more.

Columbia, Universal and the Independents

on previous page
Omar Kiam, Merle Oberon and Samuel Goldwyn discuss Kiam's designs for *The Dark Angel* (1936).

Columbia, Universal and United Artists were sometimes referred to in the thirties as 'the little three' because they did not own theatre chains. This might also refer to their importance in the area of costume design. While both Columbia and Universal had highly talented designers, there were seldom any major female stars on the lot to make them famous. Among the United Artists producers were Selznick and Goldwyn, both of whom paid enormous attention to production values, including costumes, but neither unit turned out many films.

Columbia

Hiring a costume designer was out of the question in Columbia's poverty row days of the twenties. Actresses playing leading roles were given money to go out and buy things, and Elizabeth Courteney would refit them back at the studio if

Edward Stevenson: a scene from *The Bitter Tea of General Yen* (1933), with Barbara Stanwyck.

necessary. When Frank Capra began bringing in major stars for his films, a designer was needed, and Edward Stevenson was engaged to dress Jean Harlow and Loretta Young in *Platinum Blonde* (1931) and Barbara Stanwyck and Nils Asher in *The Bitter Tea of General Yen* (1933). The studio had no sewing room and Stevenson had to install himself and a seamstress in a vacant garage.

In 1933 Robert Kalloch came in as Columbia's first contract designer. Kalloch had designed for Anna Pavlova and Mary Garden and worked with such famous couturiers as Lady Duff Gordon and Madame Frances, where he shared the designing responsibilities with Travis Banton. Kalloch's designs resembled Banton's but he was somewhat less conservative. 'Banton was pure, brilliant fashion, Kalloch was more imagination', says Edith Head. Banton's most loyal stars, Carole Lombard and Claudette Colbert, always demanded him when they loaned to the other studios, but were very happy with Kalloch's clothes at Columbia, and indeed made Universal borrow Kalloch for *Imitation of Life* (1934).. His best and most typical film was Leo MacCarey's *The Awful Truth* (1937) in which he dressed the usually dignified and stately Irene Dunne in clothes that were highly fashionable, but each change had some aspect that was exaggerated to the point of being funny. The pants of her lounging pyjamas dragged on the floor behind her for at least a foot and Dunne played this up further by acting as if they impeded her walk.

on page 156
Robert Kalloch: Carole Lombard in *20th Century* (1934). Lombard played the part of an actress in a shoddy production of a play about the civil war. The dress has the hoopskirts of the 1860s, but is otherwise purposely pure 1930s, rather tasteless and overornamented.

on page 157
Robert Kalloch: Irene Dunne in *The Awful Truth* (1937).

left
Robert Kalloch

Robert Kalloch: a sketch of Jean Arthur's wedding dress in *Arizona* (1940).

Travis Banton: Rita Hayworth in *Cover Girl* (1944) wearing the strapless dress, with a chiffon and fox wrap to soften her angularity.

When Kalloch went to MGM in 1941 Columbia studio head Harry Cohn was in no hurry to get another contract designer. Irene Saltern designed the few A pictures that came along but as the bulk of the studio output was still B pictures, they could be dressed from department stores and costume hire companies. There were no top women stars under exclusive contract and the big-name freelancing ladies always arrived with a designer. Irene Dunne brought Howard Greer for *Penny Serenade* (1941), Rosalind Russell used Travis Banton for *What a Woman* (1943) and Joan Bennett, Marlene Dietrich and Loretta Young all went to Bullocks Wilshire where Irene made exclusive designs for their films. When Rita Hayworth began to reach superstar status she too was glamourized by Irene in dresses such as a gown of white lace appliqued over nude souffle in *You Were Never Lovelier* (1942). Then Irene was contracted by MGM and Columbia had to make other arrangements. When they decided to make *Cover Girl* (1943), the studio's first Technicolor film and the best fashion picture of the war years, three designers were enlisted; Travis Banton to do most of Rita Hayworth's chic fashion, Gwen Wakeling to do the turn of the century flashback, and Muriel King to design the major supporting roles while coordinating all the purchased clothes for the endless parade of fashionable women.

'The rest of us always watched Banton because he was always a couple of years ahead of the fashion trend', says Walter Plunkett. Evening gowns in the war years usually had to be high necked and sleeved in order to cover the shoulder pads that made the silhouette of that era, but Banton used strapless gowns held up by bones or wires on Hayworth as often as possible. Dior would make this strapless bodice one of the cornerstones of his New Look, but Banton had used it

opposite
Irene: Rita Hayworth in *You Were Never Lovelier* (1942).

four years earlier. Hayworth wore such a strapless gown in *Cover Girl*, a grey chiffon, bordered with fox fur, a true Banton touch, the trimming the same colour as the dress, but in a different texture.

Banton stayed on to dress Merle Oberon in Columbia's next Technicolor feature, *A Song to Remember* (1945), while Plunkett dressed the rest of the cast. With her white skin, black hair and deep red lipstick, Oberon was a stunning subject for colour, and Banton repeated black, white and red as often as he could in her costume.

Columbia decided that it needed a contract designer again and offered the job to Jean-Louis. Like Banton's, his clothes are soft, supple and very feminine. His first assignment was *Together Again* (1944) with Irene Dunne, who liked working with him: 'I never had a designer who understood the importance of the close-up as much as Jean. He always made necklines that were different and interesting, without drawing undue attention.'

Jean-Louis' first encounter with Rita Hayworth was *Tonight and Every Night* (1945). She was pregnant and the samba 'You Excite Me' was moved up to the

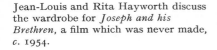

Jean-Louis and Rita Hayworth discuss the wardrobe for *Joseph and his Brethren*, a film which was never made, c. 1954.

beginning of shooting while she could still wear the bare-midriff costume Jean-Louis created. By the end, she was wearing a very flowing cloak. The film was also Jean-Louis' first excursion into Technicolor, and there were still problems. 'The Technicolor consultants wouldn't allow a real red, it had to be muddy with umber dye. We had a lot of trouble with blues too – they'd come out way too bright. I'd colour test everything and make adjustments, and then months later we'd see a release print and it was quite different. They shot both exteriors and interiors in the same costumes, and the differing lights meant that the colours didn't match.'

Jean-Louis had technical problems of a different nature in *Gilda* (1946) especially for Hayworth's now legendary 'Put the blame on Mame' number which was filmed soon after the birth of her daughter Rebecca. A cinch would have kept her from bending at the waist so Jean-Louis designed a tie which crossed over her stomach so tightly it held it in, ending with a soft bow on the hip. Keeping the strapless top up was another problem since the usual bones would have bent in the vigorous motion of the dance. Jean-Louis used bars of plastic

Jean-Louis: Rita Hayworth in the famous 'Put the Blame on Mame' dress from *Gilda* (1946).

softened over a gas flame and shaped to her dress form. No matter how she moved, they did not give way.

Jean-Louis had to use a different technique for Kim Novak. 'When she wore a strapless dress, she would not have any bones, she wanted it soft; so to keep it on, she had the idea to glue it with spirit gum. She would rip it off and it would rip her skin and tear the dress too. Not so good to fix it to shoot the day after.'

The creation of a glamorous Judy Holliday for *Born Yesterday* (1950) was Jean-Louis's most impressive achievement. 'She came in to be dressed for the test, and she was completely disinterested. We did the best we could, but it didn't look glamorous. But as soon as the camera started, that woman became all glamour. That is the great actress. The studio kept telling her to lose weight but then her mother would come up and say, "You're not eating enough!" So I

Marlene Dietrich in 1959, in one of the many gowns of souffle and brilliants that Jean-Louis has designed for her cabaret acts.

cinched her so tight she almost fainted when she stood up. Fortunately the dresses were longer then and we used dark hose.'

Only occasionally did Jean-Louis get the chance to do a costume picture and *Song Without End* (1960) was his most elaborate. But the director Charles Vidor insisted that the 1850s gowns be simplified, modernized and worn with no petti-coats. Capucine had shot only two or three sequences and Genevieve Page none at all when Vidor died and was replaced by George Cukor. For Cukor, detail is all important, so the women got their petticoats back.

Jean-Louis left in 1961 to freelance and design a highly prestigious wholesale line; and reurned to Columbia for *Guess Who's Coming to Dinner* (1967) and again for *Lost Horizon* (1971) and *Forty Carats* (1973).

Since then Columbia have hired freelance designers for their lavish costume films. In recent years Barbra Streisand has been the reason for most of these. Irene Sharaff came for *Funny Girl* (1968) and *The Way We Were* (1974), which she did with Moss Mabry. And Ray Aghatan and Bob Mackie were hired for *Funny Lady* (1975).

Universal

Today, Universal is the only Hollywood studio to have a full-time designer under contract, Edith Head, as well as several top-notch designers working in television including Leah Rhodes and Yvonne Wood. In the field of costume design as in the general operation, the long dormant giant has finally woken up.

Lucia 'Mother' Coulter was in charge of Universal's wardrobe from the very early days until she went to MGM in 1924. Then Vera West came into the fold in 1926. She designed the important production of John Stahl's *Back Street* (1932) for which Universal borrowed Irene Dunne. The approach was interesting: the ageing of the character was done through make-up and hairstyles, while the clothes remained essentially thirties, but with longer skirts and more trimming. When *Back Street* was re-made in 1941, however, the costumes, again by Vera West, with Muriel King, fell into recognizable periods.

Although Vera West designed highly attractive clothes, as soon as her actresses became important enough, they used other designers, although she dressed Marlene Dietrich in *Destry Rides Again* (1939). For instance, Irene Dunne did not use her again after *Show Boat* (1936), but went to Howard Greer. West did design all the Deanna Durbin pictures from 1937 to 1941, but after that the studio gave Durbin the highest paid designers, including Irene, Greer, Adrian and Plunkett. 'The studio adored her, they never forgot how her pictures had gotten them out of bankruptcy and whatever wardrobe she wanted, she got. She was always sweet, never petulant, but the studio was too anxious to keep her happy.'

Vera West left Universal early in 1947 to go into her own business. Walter Wanger had brought Travis Banton to Universal for the opulent *Night in Paradise* (1945) with Merle Oberon and Turnhan Bey, and he remained for a few other films. After starting *A Double Life* (1948) he was replaced by Yvonne Wood. She recalls 'They needed a dressing gown for Signe Hasso and he designed a pale chiffon with fox cuffs. But they said they didn't want that kind of thing, it had to be completely modern. Banton was so stubborn he ordered the fox from the furriers anyway. They had to take him off.' Banton was then assigned *Letter from an Unknown Woman* (1948) which was much better suited to his talents since it was a romantic period story. 'He could relate to Joan Fontaine perfectly' says Wood, 'like Dietrich and Lombard she was blonde, graceful and

Howard Greer: a costume test of Deanna Durbin in *Christmas Holiday* (1945). This was the only time Universal allowed Durbin to play a serious adult role and Greer's clothes had to ease the transition away from musical comedy. The nail head trimming on this dress was very popular during the war years.

terribly beautiful'. Orry Kelly had also been brought into Universal to design for Fontaine in another period drama, *Ivy* (1947) when he dressed her in enormous hats and dotted veils.

During the 1950s Universal had long production schedules and kept three designers very busy; Rosemary Odell, Bill Thamos and Jay Morley Jr. Most of the assignments were routine, but Ross Hunter was beginning to build a reputation for lush glamour with such stars as Ann Sheridan, Jane Wyman and Barbara Stanwyck. By the early sixties Hunter's style was called old fashioned, but it made enormous amounts of money and was a boon for the designers. Hunter gave Irene her last film jobs, but most of his productions were designed by Jean-Louis who was freelancing by then. He gave Doris Day a sophisticated glamour that revived her career, and gave Lana Turner some of her most glorious clothes.

The last of the Hunter soap-operas, *Madame X* (1965) proved to be one of the few times in recent memory a designer has had to contend with a star too glamorous for her role. Supposedly Lana Turner's mother-in-law, Constance Bennett looked about the same age. Thinner than Turner and wearing a cinch as well, Bennett warned, 'Don't try to age me with make-up. I'm going to do this the way I am.' In Jean-Louis' draped chiffons and soft sweaters, Bennett looked as beautiful as at any time in her career.

In 1968, Universal announced that it had contracted Edith Head. Between 1968 and 1975 she designed ten films for the studio (and has been loaned out for a number more) as well as tirelessly publicizing Universal products in the press and on the air.

United Artists

Through its history, United Artists has released the films of many different independent producers, including Mary Pickford, Douglas Fairbanks, Joseph Schenck, Samuel Goldwyn and David O. Selznick. Each employed designers of their own.

From the very beginnings in the early twenties, Douglas Fairbanks placed great importance on costumes. Mitchell Leisen first worked for him on *Robin Hood* (1922) and found that Western Costume, then only a few years old, had almost nothing in stock for the Middle Ages. Leisen had to make up hundreds of chain mail armours (they were knitted hemp yarn, silver leafed) each with a unique set of tabard, shield and banner. He designed hundreds of dresses for the ladies of the court and set up a small factory to make them. Many thousands of garments were also needed for *The Thief of Bagdad* (1923) an oriental fantasy for which no existing costumes would suffice (see page 114).

Mitchell Leisen also worked for Mary Pickford. He later remembers 'We really spent money on *Dorothy Vernon of Hadden Hall* (1924). Mary found out that Blanche Sweet had just made a Renaissance era film that supposedly had a gown costing $25,000. Mary wanted one that cost even more. I gave her one that cost $32,000. It was embroidered with real seed pearls.'

Pickford returned to waif roles for a while, but then she went to Howard Greer's shop for *Coquette* (1929) and asked Adrian to design her clothes for *Secrets* (1933), while Milo Anderson dressed the rest of the cast.

Joseph Schenck, who also used Pickford's studio, kept Anderson on for Joan Crawford's *Rain* (1932), and told him to furnish her two changes as cheaply as possible. Anderson bought a very simple black dress and a cheap black and white gingham suit at a department store. 'It was miles too big, except in the shoulders, so we altered the rest for her and I made the hat. I was so green then I didn't realize that when a dress is used as many days as that, there must be several

opposite
Vera West: Marlene Dietrich in *Destry Rides Again* (1939).

Mitchell Leisen: Mary Pickford in the dress embroidered with real seed pearls for *Dorothy Vernon of Hadden Hall* (1922).

Mitchell Leisen: a scene from *Dorothy Vernon of Hadden Hall* (1922) with Mary Pickford.

doubles, especially when it has to get wet and dirty. Suddenly they needed another copy and I went to the store and they didn't have any. I couldn't find the material anywhere and finally we had to paint the checks on some white cotton, which cost a fortune.'

Samuel Goldwyn used various designers on a short term basis including Coco Chanel, who came from France for three films, Adrian and Omar Kiam, who despite his name was American and rumoured to be a relative of Goldwyn's.

David O. Selznick, who joined the United Artists fold in 1934, similarly used different designers. He employed Sophie Wachner, Ernest Dryden, Travis Banton and Omar Kiam. Then, having worked with him at RKO, Selznick engaged Plunkett to design *Gone With the Wind* in 1937. Although released by MGM, the film was entirely produced at Selznick's studio. Plunkett went to Atlanta to research and through Margaret Mitchell's help, was even allowed to cut material from the seams of garments in order to find the closest possible match in modern fabrics. When Selznick began testing for Scarlett O'Hara, Plunkett had to garb each of the candidates, and used whatever dresses he could find in stock. When it looked as though Paulette Goddard would get the role, special clothes were designed and fitted and tests were made for wigs to lower her hairline.

Many tests were made of Clark Gable in various sized white hats until the one most flattering to his large head was found. Gable insisted that his usual tailor Eddie Schmidt be allowed to make his costumes; Schmidt wanted big shoulder pads to balance Gable's head and Plunkett did not. Eventually they both compromised and Plunkett says that he is 'glad of it now because it set Gable apart

166

Walter Plunkett helps Vivien Leigh with
the deep red velvet dress from *Gone with
the Wind* (1939).
left The first fitting,
right The completed dress.

from the rest of the men'. Gable's typical worldliness suited the part.

Just before shooting began, Vivien Leigh was cast in the role of Scarlett and
Plunkett had to rush to get her first costumes ready. Leigh wore the same green
sprigged dress in the first scene as she would wear in the barbecue sequence, and
when Selznick decided to reshoot the opening scene he also asked Plunkett to
design a different dress for Leigh. There were actually twenty-seven copies of the
battered calico dress Leigh wore through the burning of Atlanta sequence, a pair
in each stage of disintegration. Plunkett had to prepare several sketches for the
dress made from the green curtains before he found the idea that was satisfactory to all concerned. From there, the drapery was made to conform to the dress.
In the original Technicolor prints, the material was a brighter green than it has
appeared in the recent revivals. Of his most famous film, Plunkett says today, 'I
don't think it was my best work, or even the biggest thing I ever did. There were
more designs for *Singing in the Rain, Raintree County* and *How the West was Won*.
After all, Olivia de Havilland had only two changes before Melanie went into

Walter Plunkett: a costume sketch for Vivien Leigh's dress made from the curtains for *Gone with the Wind* (1939).

mourning! But that picture, of course, will go on forever, and that green dress, because it makes a story point, is probably the most famous costume in the history of motion pictures. So I am very glad I did it.'

Designer's Filmographies

The credits of costume designers are extremely difficult to track down. The standard works of film reference have never compiled them, they were not mentioned in trade reviews until quite recently, and before the mid-1930s were usually not mentioned in the screen credits. The following were compiled by Lee Plunkett and myself from the designers themselves (although many are deceased and others never kept any record of their work), studio records (often incomplete) and press releases. Frequently designers remembered working on films for which they received no screen credit: we took their word for it and added them to the lists. Unfortunately, for reasons of space, a number of talented designers whose output was either too small, or whose careers are just beginning, have had to be omitted. Nor have we attempted to list all the sketch artists who assisted the designers, even though such contributions were often significant. We also realize these lists are incomplete in many cases and welcome any additions our readers can provide.

The studios or producers for which the designers chiefly worked are given in parentheses after their names; exceptions are given after the title of the film.

Key to abbreviations AA – Allied Artists; AIP – American International Pictures; BV – Buena Vista; Cin – Cinerama; Col – Columbia; DeM – De Mille; EL – Eagle Lion; Emb – Embassy; FN – First National; Fox – Fox and 20th-Century Productions; MGM – Metro-Goldwyn-Mayer; Mon – Monogram; Nat Gen – National General; Par – Paramount; Pat – Pathé; Rep – Republic; RKO – RKO-Radio (Radio-Keith-Orphenum); Tob – Tobis; U – Universal and Universal International; UA – United Artists; WB – Warner Brothers.

Adrian (1926–8 DeM; 1929–52 MGM); films marked with an asterisk were done with Gile Steele.
1924: What Price Beauty (Pat). 1925 Cobra (Par); The Eagle (UA–Schenck); Her Sister From Paris (FN). 1926 Fig Leaves (Fox); For Alimony Only; Gigolo; The Volga Boatman; Young April. 1927 Almost Human; The Angel of Broadway; Chicago; The Country Doctor; Dress Parade; The Fighting Eagle; The Forbidden Woman; His Dog; The Little Adventuress; The Main Event; My Friend From India; Vanity; The Wise Wife; The Wreck of the Hesperus. 1928 The Blue Danube; Let 'Er Go Gallagher; Midnight Madness; A Ship Comes In; Skyscraper; Stand and Deliver; Walking Back; A Woman of Affairs (MGM); Dream of Love (MGM); A Lady of Chance (MGM); Love (MGM); The Masks of the Devil (MGM). 1929 The Godless Girl (DeM); The Kiss; The Last of Mrs Cheyney; Marianne; Our Modern Maidens; Devil May Care; Dynamite; A Single Man; The Single Standard; Their Own Desire; The Thirteenth Chair; The Trial of Mary Dugan; The Unholy Night; Wild Orchids. 1930 Anna Christie, die Sehnsucht jeder Frau; The Divorcee; The Floradora Girl; In Gay Madrid; The Lady of Scandal; A Lady to Love; A Lady's Morals; Let Us Be Gay; Madam Satan; Montana Moon; Not So Dumb; Our Blushing Brides; Paid; Passion Flower, Redemption; The Rogue Song; Romance; This Mad World; Their Own Desire; New Moon. 1931 The Batchelor Father; Inspiration; Laughing Sinners; Five and Ten; A Free Soul; Strangers May Kiss; The Squaw Man; Emma; The Guardsman; Flying High; Susan Lennox, Her Fall and Rise. 1932 The Wet Parade; Grand Hotel; Huddle; Strange Interlude; But the Flesh Is Weak; Arsene Lupin; Lovers Courageous; Polly of the Circus; Unashamed; Rasputin and the Empress; Red Dust; Faithless; As You Desire Me; Red Headed Woman; The Washington Masquerade; Smilin' Through; The Mask of Fu Manchu; The Son-Daughter. 1933 Men Must Fight; The Barbarian; Reunion in Vienna; Peg O' My Heart; Looking Forward; Gabriel over the White House; Made on Broadway; The White Sister; Midnight Mary; The Secret of Madame Blanche; Queen Christina; Turn Back the Clock; Dancing Lady; Beauty for Sale; Stage Mother; Dinner at Eight; When Ladies Meet; Storm at Daybreak; Hold Your Man; The Stranger's Return; Another Language; Going Hollywood; The Women in His Life; The Solitaire Man; Bombshell; Penthouse; Secrets (UA–Schenck) *w Anderson*. 1934 The Mystery of Mr X; Riptide; The Cat and the Fiddle; The Barretts of Wimpole Street; The Girl From Missouri; The Merry Widow *w A Hubert*; Outcast Lady; Sadie McKee; Men in White; Operator 13; Forsaking All Others; The Painted Veil; What Every Woman Knows. 1935 No More Ladies; Broadway Melody of 1936; After Office Hours;

Reckless; Mark of the Vampire; Anna Karenina; I Live My Life; Naughty Marietta; China Seas. 1936 San Francisco; The Great Ziegfeld; Rose Marie; Romeo and Juliet w *Oliver Messel*; The Gorgeous Hussy; Born to Dance; Camille; Love on the Run. 1937 Parnell; Maytime; The Broadway Melody of 1938; The Firefly; The Bride Wore Red; Between Two Women; Double Wedding; The Last Gangster; Mannequin; Conquest. 1938 The Girl of the Golden West; Marie Antoinette*; Love Is a Headache; The Toy Wife*; The Shopworn Angel; Three Loves Has Nancy; Sweethearts; Vacation From Love; The Shining Hour; Dramatic School. 1939 The Wizard of Oz; Ice Follies of 1939 w *Tree*; It's a Wonderful World; Broadway Serenade w *Valles*; Lady of the Tropics; Ninotchka; The Women; Balalaika; Idiot's Delight. 1940 Comrade X; Escape*; Boom Town*; Bittersweet*; The Mortal Storm*; Pride and Prejudice*; Broadway Melody of 1940 w *Valles*; New Moon; Strange Cargo; Waterloo Bridge*. 1941 When Ladies Meet; Two faced Woman; Smilin' Through*; The Feminine Touch; Lady Be Good; Dr Jekyll and Mr Hyde*; They Met in Bombay*; Blossoms in the Dust*; Rage in Heaven; Ziegfeld Girl; A Woman's Face. 1942 Woman of the Year; Keeper of the Flame. 1943 Hers to Hold (U) w *V. West*; His Butler's Sister (U) w *V. West*; Shadow of a Doubt (U) w *V. West*; Hi Diddle Diddle (UA); The Powers Girl (UA) w *R. Hubert*. 1946 Humoresque (WB) w *O'Brien*. 1947 Rope (WB). 1948 Smart Woman (Mon). 1952 Lovely to Look At w *Tony Duquette*.

Ray Aghayan
1964 Father Goose (U). 1965 The Art of Love (U); Do Not Disturb (Fox). 1966 The Glass Bottom Boat (MGM); Our Man Flint (Fox). 1967 Caprice (Fox); In Like Flint (Fox). 1969 Gaily, Gaily (UA). 1972 Lady Sings the Blues (Par) w *Bob Mackie*. 1975 Funny Lady (Col) w *Bob Mackie*.

Milo Anderson (WB)
1932 The Kid From Spain (UA–Goldwyn); Rain (UA–Schenck). 1933 Secrets (UA–Schenck) w *Adrian*; This Day and Age (Par); A Midsummer Night's Dream w *Ree*; The Story of Louis Pasteur; Oil for the Lamps of China; Alibi Ike; The Irish In Us. 1936 Anthony Adverse; Black Legion; Charge of the Light Brigade; Sing Me a Love Song; The Green Pastures; Down the Stretch; Captain Blood. 1937 The Great O'Malley; The Prince and the Pauper; The Life of Emile Zola; Midnight Court; The Great Garrick; They Won't Forget. 1938 Adventures of Robin Hood; The Amazing Dr Clitterhouse; Brother Rat; Gold Is Where You Find It; Fools for Scandal. w *Banton*. 1939 The Return of Doctor X; The Roaring Twenties; You Can't Get Away With Murder; The Cowboy Quarterback; Dust Be My Destiny; Angels Wash Their Faces; Confessions of a Nazi Spy; Dodge City; Smashing the Money Ring; Waterfront; We are Not Alone. 1940 Santa Fé Trail; They Drive by Night; King of the Lumberjacks; Invisible Stripes. 1941 High Sierra; Manpower; One Foot in Heaven; They Died With Their Boots On. 1942 Across the Pacific; The Big Shot; Juke Girl; Wings for the Eagle; Yankee Doodle Dandy; Desparate Journey; Gentleman Jim; I Was Framed; George Washington Slept Here; The Gay Sisters w *Head*; The Hard Way. 1943 Action in the North Atlantic; Edge of Darkness; The Desert Song; Thank Your Lucky Stars. 1944 Hollywood Canteen; To Have and Have Not; The Doughgirls. 1945 Conflict; Mildred Pierce; Rhapsody in Blue; San Antonio; Pillow to Post. 1946, Night and Day; Three Strangers. 1947 Life With Father; The Two Mrs Carrolls w *Head*. 1948 Johnny Belinda; Romance on the High Seas; The Woman in White. 1949 The Fountainhead; It's a Great Feeling; A Kiss in the Dark. 1950 Stage Fright; The West Point Story; Young Man With a Horn. 1951 The Blue Veil (RKO); Lullaby of Broadway; On Moonlight Bay; Painting the Clouds with Sunshine. 1952 The Story of Will Rogers; The Man Behind the Gun; Maru Maru. 1953 So Big.

Andre-Ani (MGM; films marked with an asterisk were done with Kathleen Kay and Maude Marsh).
1925 His Secretary; If Marriage Fails (FBO); Soul Mates; Sally, Irene and Mary. 1926 Bardeleys the Magnificent w *Coulter*; Beverly of Graustark; The Black Bird; Blarney; The Boy Friend*; Dance Madness* w *Erté*; The Exquisite Sinner; Exit Smiling; The Fire Brigade*; The Flaming Forest; The Gay Deceiver*; Love's Blindness*; Money Talks*; Monte Carlo*; Paris*; The Temptress w *Ree*; The Torrent* w *Ree*; Tin Hats; The Devil's Circus*; The Barrier; Upstage*; Tell It to the Marines; Valencia; The Waning Sex*; War Paint. 1927 The Flesh and the Devil; Altars of Desire*; Heaven on Earth*; Annie Laurie; Becky; The Bugle Call; California; Captain Salvation; The Demi-Bride; The Frontiersman; A Little Journey; Lovers?; The Red Mill; Rookies; Slide, Kelly Slide; Tillie the Toiler; The Understanding Heart; Women Love Diamonds. 1928 The Wind; The Crowd. 1929 The Great Gabbo (Sono–Art). 1930 The Boudoir Diplomat (U).

Adele Balkan (Fox)
1955 Seven Cities of Gold. 1956 Three Brave Men; The Girl in the Red Velvet Swing w *LeMaire*. 1957 The Way to the Gold; The Wayward Bus. 1958 The Fiend Who Walked the West; The Fly; From Hell to Texas; The Young Lions. 1959 The Blue Angel; Blue Denim; A Private's Affair. 1960 Flaming Star. 1964 John Goldfarb, Please Come Home w *Head*.

Travis Banton (1925–37 Par; 1940–1 Fox; 1945–8 U).
1917 Poppy (Select). 1925 The Dressmaker From Paris; Grounds for Divorce; The Little French Girl; The Swan. 1926 The Palm Beach Girl; The Cat's Pyjamas; The Grand Duchess and the Waiter; Dancing Mothers; The Blind Goddess; The Popular Sin; Love 'Em and Leave 'Em. 1927 Children of Divorce; Beau Sabreur; Barbed Wire; It; Rolled Stockings. 1928 Red Hair; Doomsday; The Fifty-Fifty Girl; His Tiger Lady; Interference; The Fleet's In; Docks of New York. 1929 The Man I Love; Sins of the Fathers; Abie's Irish Rose; Canary Murder Case; The Love Parade; The Dance of Life; The Wild Party; Four Feathers; Charming Sinners; The Case of Lena Smith. 1930 Fast and Loose; Slightly Scarlet; Paramount on Parade; Follow Through; Morocco; The Vagabond King; Safety in Numbers; Monte

Carlo; Let's Go Native; For the Defense; The Royal Family of Broadway. 1931 Dishonored; Girls About Town; The Mad Parade; Once a Lady; An American Tragedy; The Ladies' Man; Tarnished Lady; Up Pops the Devil; It Pays to Advertise. 1932 The Eagle and the Hawk; Blonde Venus; Evening for Sale; He Learned About Women; The Man From Yesterday; No Man of Her Own; Shanghai Express; A Farewell to Arms; Dr Jekyll and Mr Hyde; The Phantom President; Tonight Is Ours; Night After Night; Trouble in Paradise; Intimate. 1933 Brief Moments (Col) w *Kalloch*; College Humor; The Crime of the Century; Design for Living; Disgraced; From Hell to Heaven; Girl Without a Room; International House; A Lady's Profession; Midnight Club; Song of Songs; Supernatural; Terror Abroad; Three Cornered Moon; Torch Singer. 1934 All of Me; Belle of the Nineties; Bolero; Death Takes a Holiday; Enter Madame; The Great Flirtation; Here Is My Heart; Kiss and Make Up; Menace; The Scarlet Empress; Search for Beauty; You're Telling Me; Cleopatra w *Jester, Visart, Shannon Rogers and Vicki*; Now and Forever. 1935 All the King's Horses; The Bride Comes Home; The Crusades; The Devil Is a Woman; The Gilded Lily; Goin' to Town; The Lives of a Bengal Lancer; Ruggles of Red Gap; Rumba; So Red the Rose. 1936 Desire; Yours for the Asking; Valiant Is the Word for Carrie; Rose of the Rancho; The Princess Comes Across; My Man Godfrey (U); Maid of Salem; Love Before Breakfast (U); Go West, Young Man; The Big Broadcast of 1937. 1937 Angel; Champagne Waltz; Artists and Models; High, Wide and Handsome; I Met Him in Paris; Nothing Sacred (UA–Selznick) w *Plunkett*; Swing High, Swing Low. 1938 Bluebeard's Eighth Wife (Par); Fools for Scandal (WB) w *Anderson*. 1939 Made for Each Other (UA–Selznick); Eternally Yours (UA–Wanger) w *Irene*; In Name Only (RKO) w *Stevenson*; The Great Commandment (Fox). 1940 Chad Hanna; Down Argentine Way; Lillian Russell; The Mark of Zorro; The Reurn of Frank James; Tin Pan Alley; Hudson's Bay; Raffles (UA–Goldwyn); Slightly Honorable (UA). 1941 Blood and Sand; Charley's Aunt; Man Hunt; That Night in Rio; A Yank in the R.A.F.; Moon Over Miami; Western Union; How Green Was My Valley; Tobacco Road; The Great American Broadcast; Sun Valley Serenade; Belle Starr; Wild Geese Calling; Confirm or Deny w *Wakeling*. 1943 What a Woman (Col). 1944 Cover Girl (Col) w *Wakeling and Muriel King*. 1945 Scarlet Street; A Song to Remember w *Plunkett*; Wonder Man (RKO–Goldwyn); The Beautiful Cheat (Col); The Bride Wasn't Willing; The Strange Affair of Uncle Harry; This Love of Ours w *V West*. 1946 Canyon Passage (U); She Wouldn't Say Yes (Col) w *Louis*; I'll Be Yours w *V West*; Magnificent Doll w *V West*; Night in Paradise; Pirates of Monterey w *V West*; The Runaround; Tangier; Sister Kenny (RKO). 1947 The Lost Moment; Smash Up. 1948 A Double Life w *Wood*; Letter From an Unknown Wowan; The Paradine Case (Selznick); The Velvet Touch (RKO); Secret Beyond the Door. 1950 Never a Dull Moment (RKO). 1951 Valentino (Col) w *Wakeling*.

Jack Bear (Par)
1966 What Did You Do in the War, Daddy? (UA–Mirisch).

1967 Gunn; Waterhole 3. 1968 The Odd Couple; The Party (UA–Mirisch). 1969 Darling Lili w *Brooks*. 1971 Plaza Suite; The Wild Rovers (MGM).

Cecil Beaton
1948 Anna Karenina (Fox–Korda); An Ideal Husband (Fox–Korda). 1958 Gigi (MGM). 1959 The Doctor's Dilemma (MGM). 1964 My Fair Lady (WB). 1970 On a Clear Day You Can See Forever (Par) w *Arnold Scaasi*.

Marjorie Best (WB)
1949 The Adventures of Don Juan. 1950 Bright Leaf w *Rhodes*; The Flame and the Arrow. 1951 Distant Drums; I'll See You in My Dreams w *Rhodes*; On Moonlight Bay w *Anderson*. 1952 Carson City; The Crimson Pirate; The Iron Mistress; Room for One More w *Rhodes*. 1953 Blowing Wild w *Nelson*; The Charge at Feather River; The Desert Song w *Rhodes*; The Eddie Cantor Story w *Shoup*; His Majesty O'Keefe w *Liz Hennings*. 1954 King Richard and the Crusaders; The Silver Chalice. 1956 The Burning Hills; Giant w *Mabry*; Santiago w *Mabry*. 1957 Band of Angels; Shoot Out at Medicine Bend; The Story of Mankind. 1958 Born Reckless; Darby's Rangers; Fort Dobbs; Lafayette Escadrille; The Left-Handed Gun. 1959 The Hanging Tree w *Orry-Kelly*; The Miracle; The Nun's Story; Rio Bravo; Yellowstone Kelly. 1960 The Dark at the Top of the Stairs; Guns of the Timberland; Sergeant Rutledge; Sunrise at Campobello. 1961 The Comancheros (Fox); The Sins of Rachel Cade; Tender Is the Night (Fox) w *Pierre Balmain*. 1962 State Fair (Fox). 1963 Spencer's Mountain.

Donald Brooks
1963 The Cardinal (Col). 1965 The Third Day (WB). 1968 Star! (Fox). 1969 Darling Lili (Par) w *Bear*. 1975 The Drowning Pool.

Bonnie Cashin (Fox)
1944 In the Meantime, Darling; The Keys of the Kingdom; Laura; Home in Indiana. 1945 The Bullfighters; Fallen Angel; The House on 92nd Street; Junior Miss; A Tree Grows in Brooklyn; Smoky; Caribbean Mystery; Where Do We Go From Here?; Sunday Dinner for a Soldier; Diamond Horseshoe w *Nelson, Brastoff, R Hubert, LeMaire*. 1946 Anna and the King of Siam; Claudia and David; Cluny Brown; Three Little Girls in Blue; I Wonder Who's Kissing Her Now? 1947 Nightmare Alley. 1948 Cry of the City; Give My Regards to Broadway; The Iron Curtain; The Luck of the Irish; Scudda-Hoo! Scudda-Hay!; The Snake Pit; Unfaithfully Yours; The Shamrock Touch; Martin Rome. 1949 Mr Belvedere Goes to College; You're My Everything; It Happens Every Spring; I Was a Male War Bride.

Oleg Cassini (Fox)
1941 The Shanghai Gesture (UA) w *Royer*. 1946 The Razor's Edge w *LeMaire*. 1948 That Wonderful Urge. 1949 Whirlpool. 1951 Where the Sidewalk Ends; The Mating Season (Par). 1953 On the Riviera. 1963 Rampage (WB).

Ethel Chaffin (Early 20s, Par contract designer; 1925 MGM)
1925 Confessions of a Queen; The Circle; Proud Flesh; Pretty Ladies; Time the Comedian; Mike; Nothing to Wear; Lights of Old Broadway; Tower of Lies; An Exchange of Wives; The White Desert.

Coco Channel (UA–Goldwyn)
1931 Palmy Days; Tonight or Never. 1932 The Greeks Had a Word for It.

Gilbert Clark (MGM)
1927 Buttons; The Enemy; The Fair Co-ed; In Old Kentucky; Love w *R Hubert*; The Lovelorn; Man, Woman and Sin; Mockery; The Road to Romance; Tea for Three; West Point. 1928 The Actress; The Baby Cyclone; Baby Mine; Beau Broadway; Bringing up Father; A Certain Young Man; Laugh; The Mysterious Lady; The Patsy; Telling the World; Wickedness Preferred; While the City Sleeps. 1929 The Bellamy Trial; The Iron Mask (UA–Fairbanks) w *Maurice LeLoir*.

Marjorie D. Corso (AIP)
1958 Bullwhip (AA); High School Hellcats; 1959 I Mobster (Fox). 1960 Why Must I Die? 1961 The Pit and the Pendulum. 1962 The Nun and the Sergeant (UA). 1963 Beach Party; Diary of a Madman (UA); Twice Told Tales (UA). 1964 Bikini Beach; Muscle Beach Party; Pajama Party. 1965 Beach Blanket Bingo. 1966 Boy, Did I Get a Wrong Number (UA–Small).

Lucia Coulter (MGM)
1926 Lovey Mary; Bardelys the Magnificent w *Andre-Ani*. 1927 London After Midnight; Mr Wu; The Show; Spoilers of the West; Winner of the Wilderness; The Unknown. 1928 Sioux Blood; Morgan's Last Raid; The Trail of '98; Wyoming; The Adventurer; Beyond the Sierras; The Big City; The Bushranger; The Law of the Dark; Riders of the Dark; Shadows of the Night; Under the Black Eagle. 1929 The Desert Ranger; The Overland Telegraph;. 1931 The Singer of Seville. 1933 Tugboat Annie.

David Cox (MGM)
1927 The Man Who Laughs (U); Spring Fever. 1928 Across to Singapore; Circus Rookies; The Cossacks, Detectives; Diamond Handcuffs; Excess Baggage; Four Walls; Our Dancing Daughters; Rose Marie; The Smart Set; West of Zanzibar; The Cameraman. 1929 Alias Jimmy Valentine; The Broadway Melody; China Bound; The Duke Steps Out; The Flying Fleet; The Girl in the Snow; His Glorious Night; Hollywood Revue of 1929 w *Henrietta Frazer, Joe Rapf*; The Idle Rich; It's a Great Life; Madame X; A Man's Man; Navy Blues; Speedway; Spite Marriage; Tide of Empire; Where East Is East; Wise Girls; Wonder of Women. 1930 Billy the Kid; Call of the Flesh; Chasing Rainbows; Children of Pleasure; Free and Easy; The Girl Said No; Good News; Lord Byron of Broadway; Love in the Rough; Sins of the Children; Strictly Uncontentional; They Learned About Women; The

Unholy Three; Way Out West; The Woman Racket; The Ship From Shanghai. 1931 Reaching for the Moon (UA–Schenck) w *Greer*. 1933 Second Hand Wife (Fox).

Kay Dean (MGM)
1944 Blonde Fever; National Velvet w *Valles*; This Man's Navy; Two Girls and a Sailor; Music for Millions; Lost in a Harem; Barbary Coast Gent. 1945 Anchors Aweigh; Thrill of a Romance.

Mary Kay Dodson (Par)
1944 Practically Yours w *Greer*. 1945 Duffy's Tavern w *Head*; Miss Susie Slagle's w *Head*. 1946 Monsieur Beaucaire w *Steele*; O.S.S.; Our Hearts Were Growing up. 1947 Golden Earrings. 1948 The Paleface w *Steele*; The Saxon Charm (U); Whispering Smith. 1949 Alias Nick Beal; Chicago Deadline; A Connecticut Yankee in King Arthur's Court w *Steele*; Dear Wife; Sorrowful Jones; Streets of Laredo; Top o' the Morning. 1950 Captain Carey, USA. 1951 Appointment With Danger.

Donfeld (1961–2 Fox)
1961 Return to Peyton Place; Sanctuary; The Second Time Around; Wild in the Country. 1962 Bachelor Flat; Days of Wine and Roses (WB); Hemingway's Adventures of a Young Man; Mr Hobbs Takes a Vacation. 1963 Island of Love (WB); Under the Yum Yum Tree (Col). 1964 Dead Ringer (WB); Dear Heart (WB); The Outrage (WB); Robin and the Seven Hoods (WB); Viva Las Vegas (MGM). 1965 The Cincinnati Kid (MGM); The Great Race w *Head*; Joy in the Morning (MGM). 1966 The Chase (Col). 1967 Don't Make Waves (MGM); Double Trouble (MGM); Hombre (Fox); Luv (Col). 1969 The April Fools (WB); They Shoot Horses, Don't They? (WB). 1970 A Walk in the Spring Rain (Col); The Phynx (WB); The Grasshopper (Cin).

Ernest Dryden
1936 The Garden of Allah (UA–Selznick) w *Janet Couget*; The King Steps Out (Col) w *Kalloch*. 1937 Lost Horizon (Col); The Prisoner of Zenda (UA–Selznick). 1938 Dr Rhythm w *Bassett*.

Raoul Pene Du Bois (Par)
1941 Louisiana Purchase. 1943 Dixie; Happy Go Lucky. 1944 Lady in the Dark w *Head, Leisen*; Frenchmen's Creek w *Karinska*. 1945 Kitty w *Karinska*.

Eloise (Rep)
1936 The Bold Caballero; The Country Gentleman; Follow Your Heart; Happy Go Lucky; The President's Mystery. 1937 All Over Town; Dangerous Holiday; The Duke Comes Back; Escape By Night; Exiled to Shanghai; The Hit Parade; Jim Hanvey Detective; The Mandarine Mystery; Sea Racketeers; Two Wise Maids; Youth on Parole.

Erté (MGM)
1925 Time the Comedian w *Chaffin*; The Big Parade w *Chaffin*. 1926 Dance Madness w *Andre-Ani, Kay, Marsh*; The Mystic; La Bohème.

Dwight Franklin

1926 The Black Pirate (UA–Fairbanks). 1936 The Plainsman (Par) w *Natalie Visart*. 1938 The Buccaneer (Par) w *Natalie Visart*. 1947 The Exile (U); Tycoon (RKO) w *Woulfe*.

Margaret Furse

1946 Henry V (UA) w *R Furse*. 1947 Great Expectations w *Sophia Harris*. 1950 The Mudlark (Fox) w *Stevenson*. 1951 No Highway in the Sky (Fox) w *Christian Dior*; Oliver Twist (Cineguild). 1958 The Inn of the Sixth Happiness (Fox). 1960 Kidnapped (BV); Sons and Lovers (Fox). 1961 Greyfriar's Bobby (BV). 1963 The Three Lives of Thomasina (BV). 1964 Becket (Par); A Shot in the Dark (UA–Mirisch). 1965 Return From the Ashes (UA); Young Cassidy (MGM). 1966 Cast a Giant Shadow (UA). 1968 Great Catherine (WB); The Lion in Winter (Emb). 1969 Anne of a Thousand Days (U). 1970 Scrooge (Fox). 1972 Mary Queen of Scots (U). 1973 The Nelson Affair (U).

Roger Furse

1946 Henry V (UA) w *M Furse*. 1948 Hamlet. 1952 Ivanhoe (MGM). 1953 Knights of the Round Table (MGM). 1956 Helen of Troy (WB). 1957 Saint Joan (UA).

Mary Grant

1944 The Princess and the Pirate (RKO–Goldwyn). 1948 Up in Central Park (U). 1949 Bride of Vengeance (Par) w *Leisen*. 1955 We're No Angels (Par). 1956 The Vagabond King (Par). 1957 The Bachelor Party (UA). 1958 Separate Tables (UA) w *Head*. 1959 The Devil's Disciple (UA).

Howard Greer (1923–7 Par; 1932–54 RKO)

1923 The Spanish Dancer; The Cheat; Bella Donna; The Glimpses of the Moon; The White Flower; The Covered Wagon. 1924 Forbidden Paradise; The Ten Commandments w *C West*; The Female; Peter Pan; Lily of the Dust. 1925 East of the Suez; The Wanderer w *Head*; The Goose Hangs High; The Trouble With Wives; No Lives for Old. 1926 Mannequin; Good and Naughty. 1927 Hotel Imperial; It. 1928 Show People (MGM); Her Cardboard Lover (MGM); French Dressing (FN). 1929 Coquette (UA); Wall Street (Col). 1930 Hell's Angels (UA–Hughes); Prince of Diamonds (Col); Soldiers and Women (Col). 1931 Reaching for the Moon (UA–Fairbanks) w *Cox*. 1932 The Animal Kingdom w *Irene*; The Rich Are Always With Us (WB) w *Orry Kelly*; Call Her Savage (Fox). 1933 Ann Vickers w *Plunkett*; Christopher Strong w *Plunkett*; The Silver Cord w *Plunkett*. 1934 This Man Is Mine w *Plunkett*; Thirty Day Princess (Par). 1935 Dressed to Kill (Fox); Page Miss Glory (WB) w *Orry Kelly*. 1938 Bringing up Baby; Carefree; Holiday (Col) w *Kalloch*; Merrily We Live (MGM–Roach) w *Irene*. 1939 Love Affair w *Stevenson*; When Tomorrow Comes (U). 1940 My Favourite Wife. 1941 Unfinished Business (U). 1944 Follow the Boys (U) w *V West*; Practically Yours (Par) w *Dodson*; Christmas Holiday (U) w *V West, King*. 1945 Spellbound (UA–Selznick) w *Salvador Dali*. 1949 Holiday Affair. 1951 His Kind of Woman w *Woulfe*. 1954 The French Line w *Woulfe*.

Morton Haack

1958 Wild Heritage (U). 1960 Please Don't Eat the Daisies (MGM). 1961 Come September (U). 1962 Jumbo (MGM). 1964 The Unsinkable Molly Brown (MGM). 1966 Walk Don't Run (Col). 1968 Planet of the Apes (Fox). 1969 Beneath the Planet of the Apes (Fox). 1971 Escape from the Planet of the Apes (Fox).

Elizabeth Haffenden (1954–7 MGM)

1954 Beau Brummell. 1955 Quentin Durward. 1956 Bhowani Junction; Invitation to the Dance; Moby Dick (WB). 1957 The Barretts of Wimpole Street; I Accuse; Heaven Knows Mr Allison. 1960 The Sundowners (WB). 1964 Behold a Pale Horse (Col). 1965 The Amorous Adventures of Moll Flanders (Par). 1966 A Man for All Seasons (Col); The Liquidator; Arrivederci, Baby (Par). 1968 Chitty Chitty Bang Bang (UA); Half a Sixpence (Par).

Edith Head (1923–67 Par; 1968– U)

1925 The Wanderer w *Greer*. 1926 Mantrap. 1927 Wings. 1929 The Saturday Night Kid; The Virginian; Wolf Song. 1930 Along Came Youth; Only the Brave; The Santa Fé Trail. 1932 The Big Broadcast of 1932; Love Me Tonight; Undercover Man. 1933 She Done Him Wrong; Cradle Song; Hello Everybody; Sitting Pretty; Strictly Personal. 1934 Little Miss Marker. 1935 The Big Broadcast of 1936; Lives of a Bengal Lancer; Mississippi; Ruggles of Red Gap; Peter Ibbetson; Wings in the Dark. 1936 The Big Broadcast of 1937; The Jungle Princess; The Milky Way; Poppy; Woman Trap; College Holiday. 1937 The Barrier; Blond Trouble; Blossoms on Broadway; Borderland; Bulldog Drummond Comes Back; Bulldog Drummond Escapes; Bulldog Drummond's Revenge; Clarence; The Crime Nobody Saw; A Doctor's Diary; Double or Nothing; Ebb Tide; Exclusive; Forlorn River; Girl From Scotland Yard; Murder Goes to College; The Great Gambini; Hideaway Girl; Hills of Old Wyoming; Hold 'Em Navy; Hotel Haywire; Her Husband Lies; Interns Can't Take Money; John Meade's Woman w *Bridgehouse*; Last Train From Madrid; Let's Make a Million; Make Way for Tomorrow; Midnight Madonna; Mind Your Own Business; Mountain Music; Souls at Sea; Night Club Scandal; A Night of Mystery; North of the Rio Grande; On Such a Night; Outcast; Partners in Crime; Partners of the Plains; She Asked for It; She's No Lady; Sophie Lang Goes West; Texas Trail; This Way Please; Thrill of a Lifetime; True Confession; Wild Money; Turn off the Moon; Waikiki Wedding; Wells Fargo. 1938 Artists and Models Abroad; The Arkansas Traveler; Bar 20 Justice; Booloo; Born to the West; Bulldog Drummond in Africa; Bulldog Drummond's Peril; Campus Confessions; Coconut Grove; Professor Beware; Prison Farm; Pride of the West; Men With Wings; Love on Toast; Little Orphan Annie; King of Alcatraz; In Old Mexico; Illegal Traffic; Hunted Men; Her Jungle Love; Heart of Arizona; Give Me a Sailor; The Frontiersman; College Swing; Ride a Crooked Mile; Say It in French; Scandal Sheet; Sing You Sinners; Tropic Holiday; Touchdown, Army; Tom Sawyer Detective; Tip-off Girls; Thanks for the Memory; The Texans; Sons of the Legion; Spawn of the North; Stolen

Heaven. 1939 Arrest Bulldog Drummond; All Women Have Secrets; Honeymoon in Bali; Heritage of the Desert; Back Door to Heaven; Beau Geste; Boy Trouble; The Great Victor Herbert; Grand Jury Secrets; The Gracie Allen Murder Case; Geronimo; Disputed Passage; Disbarred; Death of a Champion; The Cat and the Canary; Cafe Society; Bulldog Drummond's Secret Police; Bulldog Drummond's Bride; Night Work; The Night of Nights; Hotel Imperial; I'm From Missouri; Invitation to Happiness; Island of Lost Men; The Lady's From Kentucky; Law of the Pampas; The Light That Failed; The Llano Kid; The Magnificent Fraud; Man About Town; Million Dollar Legs; Never Say Die; $1,000 a Touchdown; Undercover Doctor; This Man Is News; Television Spy; Sudden Money; St Louis Blues; Some Like It Hot; The Star Maker; Rulers of the Sea; Our Leading Citizen; Our Neighbors, the Carters; Paris Honeymoon; Persons in Hiding; What a Life; Unmarried; Zaza. 1940 Adventure in Diamonds; Buck Benny Rides Again; Cherokee Strip; Christmas in July; Comin' Round the Mountain; Dancing on a Dime; Doctor Cyclops; Emergency Squad; The Farmer's Daughter; French Without Tears; Geronimo; The Ghost Breakers; Rhythm on the River; Remember the Night; Rangers of Fortune; Queen of the Mod; Quarterback; A Parole Fixer; Opened by Mistake; A Night at Earl Carrols; Golden Gloves; The Great McGinty; I Want a Divorce; Love They Neighbor; Moon Over Burma; Mystery Sea Raider; Road to Singapore; Safari; Seventeen; The Show Down; Stagecoach War; Those Were the Days; Women Without Names; The Way of all Flesh; Untamed; Typhoon; Three Men From Texas. 1941 Aloma of the South Seas; Among the Living; Life With Henry; Las Vegas Nights; The Lady Eve; Kiss the Boys Goodbye; I Wanted Wings; Hold Back the Dawn; Bahama Passage; Birth of the Blues; Buy Me That Town; Caught in the Draft; Doomed Caravan; Flying Blind; Forced Landing; Glamour Boy; Henry Aldrich for President; West Point Widow; World Première; You're the One; You Belong to Me (Col); Ball of Fire (RKO–Goldwyn); Skylark *w Irene*; Kiss the Boys Goodbye; Sullivan's Travels; Road to Zanzibar; Here Comes Mr Jordan (Col); There's Magic in Music; Virginia; I Wanted Wings; Shepherd of the Hills; Reaching for the Sun; New York Town; One Night in Lisbon. 1942 The Gay Sisters (WB) *w Anderson*; The Great Man's Lady; I Married a Witch (UA–Cinema Guild) The Major and the Minor; The Road to Morocco; This Gun for Hire; Beyond the Blue Horizon; The Remarkable Andrew; The Fleet's in; Young and Willing (UA–Cinema Guild); My Favourite Blonde; Are Husbands Necessary?; Holiday Inn; The Glass Key; Star Spangled Rhythm; Lucky Jordan. 1943 Flesh and Fantasy (U) *w V West*; True to Life (Par); Lady of Burlesque (UA–Stromberg) *w Natalie Visart*; No Time for Love *w Irene*; The Crystal Ball (UA–Cinema Guild); China; Salute for Three; Five Graves to Cairo; Riding High; Let's Face It; Hostages; Tender Comrade (RKO) *w Renie*. 1944 And Now Tomorrow; Going My Way; Here Come the Waves; I Love a Soldier; I'll Be Seeing You (Vanguard); Our Hearts Were Young and Gay; The Uninvited; Standing Room Only; Lady in the Dark *w Du Bois, Leisen*; Rainbow Island; Double Indemnity; Ministry of Fear; And the Angels Sing; Hour Before Dawn. 1945 The Affairs of Susan; The Bells of St Mary's (RKO); Christmas in Connecticut (WB) *w Anderson*; Duffy's Tavern *w Dodson*; Incendiary Blonde; The Lost Weekend; Love Letters; Masquerade in Mexico; A Medal for Benny; Miss Susie Slagle's *w Dodson*; Out of This World; The Road to Utopia; The Stork Club. 1946 The Blue Dahlia; My Reputation (WB) *w Rhodes*; Notorious (RKO); The Strange Love of Martha Ivers; To Each His Own; The Virginian; The Well-Groomed Bride; Blue Skies *w Waldo Angelo*; The Perfect Marriage; Cross My Heart; The Bride Wore Boots; California. 1947 The Road to Rio; The Two Mrs Carrolls (WB) *w Anderson*; Welcome Stranger; My Favorite Brunette; Desert Fury; I Walk Alone; Where There's Life; Wild Harvest; Perils of Pauline; Variety Girl; Blaze of Noon; Ramrod (UA–Enterprise). 1948 The Big Clock; The Emperor Waltz *w Steele*; A Foreign Affair; Miss Tatlock's Millions; The Night Has a Thousand Eyes; Rachel and the Stranger (RKO); Sorry Wrong Number (Par); Arch of Triumph (UA–Enterprise); Dream Girl; My Own True Love; Beyond Glory; Sainted Sisters; So Evil My Love; Isn't It Romantic; June Bride (WB) *w Rhodes*. 1949 The Heiress *w Steele*; Red, Hot and Blue; Rope of Sand; My Friend Irma; The Great Lover; The Great Gatsby; Beyond the Forest (WB). 1950 Copper Canyon *w Steele*; Mr Music; My Foolish Heart (RKO–Goldwyn) *w Wills*; My Friend Irma Goes West; Riding High; Samson and Delilah *w Steele, Jeakins, Wakeling, Elois Jenssen*; Sunset Boulevard; Paid in Full; September Affair; All About Eve (Fox) *w LeMaire*. 1951 The Big Carnival; Branded; Detective Story; Here Comes the Groom; The Lemon Drop Kid; Payment on Demand (RKO); A Place in the Sun; That's My Boy. 1952 Carrie; The Greatest Show on Earth *w Jeakins, White*; Jumping Jacks; Just For You *w Wood*; My Favorite Spy; Sailor Beware; Son of Paleface; Something to Live for. 1953 The Caddy; Come Back Little Sheba; Off Limits; Road to Bali; Roman Holiday; Sangaree; Scared Stiff: Shane; The Stooge; Red Garters *w Wood*; The Stars Are Singing. 1954 Elephant Walk; Here Come the Girls; Knock on Wood; Living It up; Money From Home; The Naked Jungle; Rear Window; Sabrina; White Christmas; The Country Girl; About Mrs Leslie. 1955 Artists and Models; The Bridges at Toko-Ri; The Desperate Hours; The Far Horizon; The Girl Rush; Hell's Island; Lucy Gallant; The Rose Tatoo; Run For Cover; The Seven Little Foys; Strategic Air Command; Three Ring Circus; To Catch a Thief; The Trouble With Harry; You're Never Too Young. 1956 Anything Goes; The Birds and the Bees; The Court Jester *w Wood*; Hollywood or Bust; The Leather Saint; The Man Who Knew Too Much; The Mountain; Pardners; The Proud and the Profane; The Rainmaker; The Scarlet Hour; The Search for Bridey Murphey; That Certain Feeling; The Lonely Man. 1957 Beau James; The Buster Keaton Story; The Delicate Delinquent; The Devil's Hairpin; Fear Strikes Out; Funny Face *w Hubert de Givinchy*; Gunfight at the O.K. Corral; Hear Me Good; The Joker is Wild; Loving You; The Sad Sack; Short Cut to Hell; The Ten Commandments *w Jeakins, Jester John Jensen, Arnold Friberg*; The Tin Star; Three Violent, People; Wild Is the Wind. 1958 As Young as We Are; The Buccaneer *w Jester*; The Geisha Boy; Hot Spell; Houseboat;

Macaibo; The Matchmaker; Rock-A-Bye Baby; Seperate Tables (UA–Hecht Hill Lancaster) w *Grant*; St Louis Blues; Teacher's Pet; Vertigo; Witness for the Prosecution (UA). 1959 Alias Jesse James (UA); The Black Orchid; Career; A Hole in the Head (UA); The Jayhawkers; That Kind of Woman; The Five Pennies. 1960 The Facts of Life (UA) w *Stevenson*; Cinderfella; Heller in Pink Tights; Pepe; The Rat Race; A Visit to a Small Planet. 1961 All in a Night's Work; Breakfast at Tiffany's w *Hubert de Givinchy, Pauline Trigere*; The Errand Boy; The Ladies' Man; Man-Trap; On the Double; The Pleasure of His Company; Pocketful of Miracles (UA) w *Plunkett*; Summer and Smoke. 1962 The Counterfeit Traitor; Hatari; It's Only Money; My Geisha; Too Late Blues; Who's Got the Action?; The Man Who Shot Liberty Valance. 1963 The Birds (U); Come Blow Your Horn; Critic's Choice; Donovan's Reef; Fun in Acapulco; A Girl Named Tamiko; Hud; I Could Go on Singing (UA); My Six Loves; A New Kind of Love; The Nutty Professor; Papa's Delicate Condition; Who's Minding The Store?; Wives and Lovers. 1964 The Carpetbaggers; The Disorderly Orderly; A House Is Not a Home (Emb); Love With the Proper Stranger; Man's Favorite Sport; Marnie; The Patsy; Roustabout; Sex and the Single Girl (WB) w *Norman Norell*; What a Way to Go! (Fox) w *Mabry*; Where Love Has Gone. 1965 Boeing, Boeing; The Family Jewels; The Hallelujah Trail (UA); Harlow w *Mabry*; John Goldfarb, Please Come Home (Fox) w *Balkan*; Love Has Many Faces (Col); The Sons of Katie Elder; Sylvia; The Yellow Rolls-Royce w *Castello, Pierre Cardin*; The Slender Thread. 1966 Assault on a Queen; The Last of the Secret Agents; Not With My Wife You Don't!; The Oscar (Emb); Paradise, Hawaiian Style; Penelope (MGM); The Swinger; This Property Is Condemned; Torn Curtain (U); Waco; Inside Daisy Clover (WB) w *Thomas*. 1967 Barefoot in the Park; The Caper of the Golden Bulls (Emb); Chuka; Easy Come, Easy Go; Warning Shot; Hotel (WB) w *Shoup*. 1968 In Enemy Country; The Pink Jungle; The Secret War of Harry Frigg; What's So Bad About Feeling Good? 1969 Topaz; Story of a Woman; Eye of the Cat; The Lost Man; Butch Cassidy and the Sundance Kid (Fox); Airport. 1970 Sweet Charity. 1971 Red Sky at Morning; Hammersmith is Out (EMI). 1973 Judge Roy Bean (Nat Gen); Pete 'n Tillie (U); A Doll's House (World Film Services). 1974 The Don Is Dead; Ash Wednesday (Par). 1975 Airport 75; Rooster Cogburn; The Man Who Would Be King (Col); The Great Waldo Pepper; Gable and Lombard.

Herschel (1936–43 Fox; 1951–3 MGM)
1936 Career Woman; Charlie Chan at the Opera; Back to Nature; Can This Be Dixie?; Charlie Chan at the Race Track; Crack-Up; Fifteen Maiden Lane; Pepper; Star for a Night; Thank You, Jeeves; The Holy Terror; Thirty Six Hours to Kill. 1937 Charlie Chan at the Olympics; Woman Wise; Step Lively; Jeeves; That I May Love; Thank You, Mr Moto; Think Fast, Mr Moto; Sing and Be Happy; Ali Baba Goes to Town w *Wakeling*; Angel's Holiday; Big Town Girl; Born Reckless; The Midnight Taxi; She Had to Eat; Time Out for Romance; The Lady Escapes; Laughing at Trouble; Hot Water; Dangerously Yours; Fair Warning;

Forty Five Fathers; Charlie Chan on Broadway; One Mile From Heaven; Off to the Races; Borrowing Trouble. 1938 Keep Smiling; Passport Husband; Time Out for Murder; Battle of Broadway; Five of a Kind w *Myron*; International Settlement; Island in the Sky; Meet the Girls; Mr Moto Takes a Chance; Mysterious Mr Moto; Road Demon; Sharpshooters. 1939 Winner Takes All; The Arizona Wildcats; Twenty Thousand a Year; Mr Moto in Danger Island; Charlie Chan at Treasure Island; The Escape; Hollywood Cavalcade; Pardon Our Nerve; Charlie Chan in the City of Darkness; The Cisco Kid and the Lady; Frontier Marshall; The Honeymoon's Over; Heaven with a Barbed Wire Fence; Mr Moto Takes a Vacation. 1940 The Gay Caballero; Charlie Chan at the Wax Museum; Private Practice of Michael Shane; Earthbound; Dead Men Tell; Cowboy and the Blonde; Street of Memories; Viva Cisco Kid; Sailor's Lady; Manhattan Heartbeat; The Man Who Wouldn't Talk; Charter Pilot; Jennie. 1941 Ride Kelly Ride; Great Guns; Murder Among Friends; Private Nurse; Sleepers West; Last of the Duanes; Charlie Chan in Rio; Marry the Boss's Daughter; We Go Fast; Forward March; Young People; A Perfect Snob; Castle in the Desert; On the Sunny Side; Dead Men Tell; Small Town Deb; Dance Hall. 1942 Dr Renalt's Secret; Manila Calling; That Other Woman; My Friend Flicka; The Brasher Doubloon; Ten Dollar Raise; The Man in the Trunk; Right to the Heart; Sundown Jim; The Mad Martindales; The Night Before the Divorce; Berlin Correspondent; A-Haunting We Will Go; Blue, White and Perfect. 1943 He Hired the Boss; Quiet Please, Murder; Dixie Dugan. 1951 Quo Vadis. 1953 Give a Girl a Break w *Rose*; Julius Caesar; Latin Lovers w *Rose*. 1954 The Prodigal.

Ali Hubert
1919 Madame Du Barry (UFA). 1920 Anna Boleyn (UFA); Sumurun (UFA). 1927 The Student Prince (MGM) w *Eric Locke*. 1928 The Patriot (Par). 1934 The Merry Widow (MGM) w *Adrian*. 1937 The Life of Emile Zola (WB) w *Anderson*. 1938 Blockade (UA–Wanger) w *Irene*.

René Hubert (1925–6 Par; 1927–31 MGM; 1931–5 and 1943–64 Fox; 1936–41 UA–Korda)
1925 Madame Sans Gene; Coast of Folly; Stage Struck; The Swan. 1926 Beau Geste; The Untamed Lady. 1927 Adam and Evil; After Midnight; Body and Soul; The Callahans and the Murphys; Foreign Devils; Frisco Sally Levy; Love w *Clark*; Loves of Sunya (UA–Schenck); On Ze Boulevard; Mr Wu; Quality Street; Twelve Miles Out. 1928 The Wind. 1929 Asphalt; The Bridge of San Luis Rey; Nina Petrowna (UFA); Manolescu (UFA). 1930 Min and Bill; Those Three French Girls; Reducing; The Trial of Mary Dugan; The Great Meadow; War Nurse; Sous les Toits de Paris (TOG); Die Drei von der Tankstelle (UFA). 1931 Indiscreet (UA); A Nous la Liberté (Tob); Gentlemen's Fate; Shipmates; Stepping Out; Just a Gigolo; Parlor Bedroom and Bath; A Tailor Made Man (Fox); Guilty Hands (Fox); Son of India (Fox); The Great Lover (Fox); The Sin of Madelon Claudet (Fox). 1932 Flesh. 1933 Waltzkrieg (UFA). 1934 Music in the Air; Elinor Norton; Servant's Entrance. 1935 Curly Top; The

Daring Young Man; Doubting Thomas; The Farmer Takes a Wife; Here's to Romance; Lottery Lover; Orchids to You; Our Little Girl; Spring Tonic; Under the Pampas Moon. 1936 The Ghost Goes West; Things to Come. 1937 The Dark Journey; Fire Over England; Knight Without Armour; Under the Red Robe (Fox); Wings of the Morning (Fox). 1938 The Divorce of Lady X; Drums; The Return of the Scarlet Pimpernel; A Yank at Oxford (MGM). 1939 The Four Feathers. 1940 Over the Moon. 1941 Father Takes a Wife (RKO); The Flame of New Orleans (U); New Wine (UA); That Hamilton Woman. 1942 The Pride of the Yankees (RKO–Goldwyn). 1943 Claudia; Happy Land; Heaven Can Wait; Holy Matrimony; Paris After Dark; The Powers Girl (UA) w *Adrian*; Song of Bernadette; Sweet Rosie O'Grady. 1944 Buffalo Bill; Irish Eyes Are Smiling; It Happened Tomorrow (UA); Jane Eyre; Lifeboat; The Lodger; Pin-Up Girl; The Sullivans; Tampico; Wilson. 1945 Captain Eddie; Diamond Horshoe w *Cashin, Nelson, Brastoff, LeMaire*; Hangover Square; Nob Hill; A Royal Scandal; The Spider; State Fair. 1946 Centennial Summer; Dragonwyck; My Darling Clementine; 13 Rue Madeleine; Wake Up and Dream. 1947 Carnival in Costa Rica; Forever Amber; The Foxes of Harrow; The Late George Apley; Moss Rose. 1948 Fury at Furnace Creek; Green Grass of Wyoming; That Lady in Ermine; When My Baby Smiles at Me. 1949 The Beautiful Blonde From Bashful Bend; The Fan; Oh, You Beautiful Doll. 1950 Broken Arrow; Ticket to Tomahawk. 1954 Desirée. 1956 Anastasia. 1959 The Journey (MGM). 1962 The Four Horsemen of the Apocalypse (MGM) w *Orry Kelly, Plunkett*. 1964 The Visit.

Irene (1942–50 MGM; 1960–3 U)
1932 The Animal Kingdom (RKO) w *Greer*. 1933 Goldie Gets Along (RKO); Flying Down to Rio (RKO) w *Plunkett*. 1936 The Unguarded Hour (MGM). 1937 Vogues of 1938 (UA–Wanger) w *Kiam*. 1938 Algiers (UA–Wanger); Merrily We Live (MGM–Roach) w *Greer*; There Goes My Heart (UA–Roach); Trade Winds (UA–Wanger) w *Taylor*; Vivacious Lady (RKO) w *Newman*; You Can't Take It With You (Col) w *Newman*; Blockade (UA–Wanger) w *A Hubert*. 1939 Bachelor Mother (RKO); Eternally Yours (UA–Wanger); Intermezzo (UA–Selznick); Topper Takes a Trip (UA–Roach); Midnight (Par) w *Head*; The Housekeeper's Daughter (UA–Roach). 1940 Arise My Love (Par) w *Head*; Lucky Partners (RKO) w *Renie*; Seven Sinners (U) w *V West*; The House Across the Bay (UA–Roach). 1941 That Uncertain Feeling (UA–Lesser); Skylark (Par) w *Head*; Sundown (UA) w *Plunkett*. 1942 The Lady Is Willing (Col); The Palm Beach Story (Par) w *Head*; Reunion in France; Take a Letter Darling (Par) w *Leisen*; The Talk of the Town (Col); They All Kissed the Bride (Col); To Be or Not to Be (UA) w *Plunkett*; You Were Never Lovelier (Col); Three Hearts for Julia. 1943 Song of Russia; The Heavenly Body; Cry Havoc; Lost Angel; The Youngest Profession; Above Suspicion; Swing Shift Masie; Thousands Cheer; Slightly Dangerous; The Human Comedy; The Man From Down Under; Dr Gillespie's Criminal Case; Whistling in Brooklyn. 1944 Between Two Women; Mrs Parkington w *Valles*; The Seventh

Cross; Two Girls and a Sailor; An American Romance; Andy Hardy's Blonde Trouble; Nothing But Trouble; A Guy Named Joe; See Here Private Hargrove; Masie Goes to Reno; The White Cliffs of Dover. 1945 Adventure; The Sailor Takes a Wife; Thrill of a Romance; Weekend at the Waldorf; Yolanda and the Thief w *Sharaff*. 1946 Bad Bascomb; Easy to Wed w *Valles*; The Green Years w *Valles*; The Postman Always Rings Twice; Holiday in Mexico w *Valles*; Undercurrent; Two Smart People w *Valles*; Courage of Lassie; Boy's Ranch; The Lady in the Lake; Love Laughs at Andy Hardy; The Secret Heart; No Leave No Love. 1947 Fiesta w *Plunkett*; This Time For Keeps w *Valles*; The Arnelo Affair; The Beginning or the End; Undercover Maisie; Dark Delusion; High Barbaree; Desire Me; 10th Avenue Angel; If Winter Comes. 1948 Cass Timberlane; Easter Parade w *Valles*; Julia Misbehaves; On an Island With You; State of the Union; B.F.'s Daughter. 1949 The Barkleys of Broadway; In the Good Old Summertime w *Valles*; Neptune's Daughter; The Great Sinner w *Valles*; The Sun Comes Up; Malaya w *Valles*; The Shadow on the Wall; The Scene of the Crime. 1950 Key to the City. 1960 Midnight Lace. 1962 Lover Come Back. 1963 A Gathering of Eagles.

Dorothy Jeakins (1952–4 Fox)
1948 Joan of Arc (RKO–Sierra) w *Karinska*. 1949 Samson and Delilah (Par) w *Steele, Head, Wakeling, Elois Jenssen*. 1952 Belles on their Toes; The Big Sky (RKO); The Grestest Show on Earth (Par) w *Head, White*; Les Miserables; Lure of the Wilderness; My Cousin Rachel; The Outcasts of Poker Flat; Stars and Stripes Forever; Treasure of the Golden Condor. 1953 Beneath the 12 Mile Reef; City of Badmen; Inferno; The Kid From Left Field; Niagara; Titanic; White Witch Doctor. 1954 Three Coins in the Fountain. 1956 Friendly Persuasion (AA). 1957 The Ten Commandments (Par) w *Head, Jester, John Jensen, Arnold Friberg*. 1958 South Pacific. 1959 Green Mansions (MGM). 1960 Elmer Gantry (UA); Let's Make Love; The Unforgiven (UA). 1961 The Children's Hour (UA–Mirisch). 1962 All Fall Down (MGM); The Music Man (WB). 1964 The Best Man (UA); Ensign Pulver (WB); The Night of the Iguana (MGM). 1965 The Fool Killer (Landau); The Sound of Music. 1966 Any Wednesday (WB); Hawaii (UA); Violent Journey (AIP). 1967 The Film Flam Man; Reflections in a Golden Eye (WB). 1968 Finian's Rainbow (WB); The Fixer (MGM). 1969 True Grit (Par); The Molly MacGuires (Par). 1970 Little Big Man (Nat Gen). 1974 Young Frankenstein; The Iceman Cometh (American Film Theatre). 1975 The Hindenburg (U).

Ralph Jester (Par)
1934 Cleopatra w *Banton, Natalie Visart, Shannon Rogers, Vicki*. 1936 The Crusades w *Banton, Natalie Visart, Shannon Rogers*. 1957 Omar Khayyam; The Ten Commandments w *Head, Jeakins, John Jensen, Arnold Friberg*. 1958 The Buccaneer w *Head, John Jensen*.

Anna Hill Johnstone (WB)
1955 East of Eden. 1956 Baby Doll. 1957 Edge of the City (MGM); A Face in the Crowd. 1960 Wild River (Fox). 1961

Splendour in the Grass. 1962 David and Lisa (Continental). 1963 America, America; Ladybug, Ladybug (UA). 1964 Fail Safe (Col). 1965 Harvey Middleman, Fireman (Col); The Pawnbroker (AA). 1966 The Group (UA). 1968 Bye Bye Braverman; The Night They Raided Minsky's (UA); The Subject Was Roses (MGM); The Swimmer (Col). 1969 Alice's Restaurant (UA). 1970 Cotton Comes to Harlem (UA). There Was a Crooked Man. 1974 The Taking of Pelham 1 2 3 (Par); Serpico (Par).

Robert Kalloch (Col)

1933 Brief Moments w *Banton*; Child of Manhattan; The Circus Queen Murder; Cocktail Hour; Master of Men; My Woman; When Strangers Marry; The Woman I Stole; Lady for a Day. 1934 Before Midnight; Black Moon; Broadway Bill; The Captain Hates the Sea; Imitation of Life (U); Sisters Under the Skin; One Night of Love; It Happened One Night. 1935 Let's Live Tonight; Love Me Forever. 1936 The King Steps Out w *Dryden*. 1937 The Awful Truth; It's All Yours; Let's Get Married; The Game That Kills; Murder in Greenwich Village; I'll Take Romance; Paid to Dance; Racketeers in Exile; Life Begins With Love. 1938 Holiday w *Greer*; There's Always a Woman; I am the Law; The Lady Objects; She Married an Artist; Squadron of Honor; Start Cheering; Women in Prison; Joy of Living (RKO) w *Stevenson*. 1939 The Amazing Mr Williams; Golden Boy; The Lady and the Mob; Mr Smith Goes to Washington; Only Angels Have Wings; Blondie Takes a Vacation; Good Girls Go to Paris; Let Us Live. 1940 Angels Over Broadway; Arizona; His Girl Friday; The Lone Wolf Strikes; Music in My Heart. 1941 Babes on Broadway (MGM); Honky Tonk; Johnny Eager; Dr Kildare's Victory; Design for Scandal; The Vanishing Virginian; The Bugle Sounds w *Steele*; Mr and Mrs North; The People vs Dr Kildare; The Getaway; Married Bachelor; Dr Kildare's Wedding Day; Life Begins For Andy Hardy; H.M. Pulham Esq. w *Steele*. 1942 Crossroads; Mrs Miniver w *Steele*; Random Harvest; Ship Ahoy; Somewhere I'll Find You; Tortilla Flat; Calling Dr Gillespie; Her Cardboard Lover; I Married an Angel w *Motley*; Cairo; The War Against Mrs Hadley; Panama Hattie; Maisie Gets Her Man; Rio Rita w *Steele*; Sunday Punch; Pacific Rendezvous; For Me and My Gal w *Steele*; Eyes in The Night; White Cargo; Journey for Margaret.

Madame Barbara Karinska

1944 Gaslight (MGM); Kismet (MGM). 1945 Kitty (Par) w *Du Bois*. 1947 Unconquered (Par) w *Wakeling*. 1948 Joan of Arc (RKO–Sierra) w *Jeakins*. 1952 Hans Christian Anderson (RKO–Goldwyn) w *Wills, Clave*. 1967 A Midsummer Night's Dream (Show).

Rita Kaufman (Fox)

1933 Hoopla; My Weakness; The Power and the Glory; State Fair; Doctor Bull. 1934 As Husbands Go; Carolina; Grand Canary; The World Moves On; All Men Are Enemies; Change of Heart; David Harum; The Great Hospital Mystery; Mr Skitch; Now I'll Tell; Springtime for Henry; Stand Up and Cheer; Such Men Are Dangerous.

Kathleen Kay (MGM; all films w *Marsh* unless noted.)

1926 Beverly of Graustark; The Boy Friend; Brown of Harvard; Dance Madness; The Fire Brigade; The Gay Deceiver; Love's Blindness; Money Talks; Monte Carlo; Paris; There You Are!; The Torrent; Upstage; The Waning Sex. 1927 Altars of Desire; Heaven on Earth; Chain Lightning (Fox) w *Stevenson*; The Heart of a Salome (Fox) w *Stevenson*.

Orry Kelly (1932–44 WB; 1947–50 U)

1932 The Rich Are Always With Us w *Greer*; So Big; You Said a Mouthful; I am a Fugitive From a Chain Gang; The Crash; The Match King; One Way Passage; Week-End Marriage. 1933 Captured; Central Airport; Convention City; Ex-Lady; Female; 42nd Street w *Anderson*; Hard to Handle; The House on 56th Street; The Keyhole; Lady Killer; The Narrow Corner; The Picture Snatcher; Private Detective 62; Voltaire; The Working Man; The Mystery of the Wax Museum. 1934 As the Earth Turns; British Agent; The Circus Clown; Dames; Dark Hazard; Desirable; Dr Monica; The Dragon Murder Case; Easy to Love; Fashions of 1934; The Firebird; Flirtation Walk; Happiness Ahead; Harold Teen; Here Comes the Navy; Hi Nellie; Housewife; I Am a Thief; Kansas City Princess; The Key; Madame Du Barry; The Merry Frinks; Merry Wives of Reno; Midnight Alibi; Murder in the Clouds; The Personality Kid; Return of the Terror; Smarty; Wonder Bar; Babbitt. 1935 Bordertown; Bright Lights; Broadway Gondolier; Broadway Hostess; Dangerous; The Frisco Kid; G Men; The Girl from Tenth Avenue; I Found Stella Parish; In Caliente; Living on Velvet; Miss Pacific Fleet; Page Miss Glory w *Greer*; The Payoff; Shipmates Forever; Stars Over Broadway; Sweet Adeline; The Widow From Monte Carlo; The Woman in Red; Front Page Woman; The Goose and the Gander; Special Agent; Stranded. 1936 China Clipper; Colleen; Freshman Love; Give Me Your Heart; Gold Diggers of 1937; The Golden Arrow; Hearts Divided; I Married a Doctor; Isle of Fury; Jailbreak; The Law in Her Hands; Murder by an Aristocrat; The Petrified Forest; Polo Joe; Satan Met a Lady; The Singing Kid; Snowed Under; Stage Struck; Stolen Holiday; Times Square Playboy; The White Angel; Cain and Mabel. 1937 Another Dawn; Call It a Day; First Lady; The Go Getter; Green Light; Hollywood Hotel; It's Love I'm After; Kid Galahad; The King and the Chorus Girl; Marked Woman; That Certain Woman; Tovarich; Confession; Ever Since Eve. 1938 Angels With Dirty Faces; Four Daughters w *Shoup*; Four's a Crowd; Jezebel; My Bill; Secrets of an Actress; The Sisters; Comet Over Broadway; Women Are Like That. 1939 Dark Victory; Juarez; King of the Underworld; The Oklahoma Kid; The Old Maid; The Private Lives of Elizabeth and Essex; Women in the Wind; On Your Toes. 1940 All This and Heaven Too; The Letter; The Sea Hawk. 1941 The Bride Came C.O.D.; The Great Lie; King's Row; The Little Foxes (RKO–Goldwyn); The Maltese Falcon; The Man Who Came to Dinner; The Strawberry Blonde. 1942 Casablanca; In This Our Life; Now Voyager. 1943 Old Acquaintance; This Is the Army; Watch on the Rhine; The Constant Nymph; Mission to Moscow. 1944 Arsenic and Old Lace; Mr Skeffington. 1945 The Corn Is Green; The Dolly

Sisters (Fox). 1946 A Stolen Life. 1947 The Shocking Miss Pilgrim (Fox); Ivy; Mother Wore Tights (Fox); Something in the Wind; A Woman's Revenge. 1948 For the Love of Mary; Larceny w *Odell*; One Touch of Venus; Rogues' Regiment. 1949 Family Honeymoon; East of Java; The Lady Gambles; Johnny Stool Pidgeon; Undertow; Woman in Hiding; Take One False Step. 1950 Deported; Under the Gun; Behave Yourself (WB). 1951 An American in Paris (MGM) w *Plunkett, Sharaff*; Harvey (U); The Lady Says No! (UA). 1952 Pat and Mike (MGM); The Star (Fox). 1953 I Confess (WB). 1955 Oklahoma! (Magna) w *Motley*. 1957 Les Girls (MGM). 1958 Auntie Mame (WB); Too Much, Too Soon (WB). 1959 The Hanging Tree (WB) w *Best*; Some Like It Hot (UA–Mirisch). 1961 A Majority of One (WB). 1962 The Chapman Report (WB); The Four Horsemen of the Apocalypse (MGM) w *R Hubert, Plunkett*; Gypsy (WB); Sweet Bird of Youth (MGM); Two for the Seesaw (UA–Mirisch). 1964 In The Cool of the Day (MGM) w *Pierre Balmain*; Irma La Douce (UA–Mirisch).

Marion Herwood Keyes (MGM)

1944 Between Two Women; The Thin Man Goes Home; Mrs Parkington; Marriage Is a Private Affair. 1945 The Valley of Decision; Without Love; Adventure; A Letter for Evie; The Clock; Keep Your Powder Dry; The Picture of Dorian Gray w *Valles*; Her Highness and the Bellboy w *Valles*; The Hidden Eye. 1946 Easy to Wed w *Valles*; The Hoodlum Saint w *Valles*. 1947 Body and Soul (UA–Enterprise).

Omar Kiam (UA–Goldwyn)

1933 Dinner at Eight (MGM) w *Adrian*; Reunion in Vienna (MGM). 1934 Kid Millions; The Mighty Barnum; We Live Again. 1935 Barbary Coast; Call of the Wild (UA–20th); Cardinal Richelieu (UA–20th); Clive of India (UA–20th); The Dark Angel; Folies Bergères (UA–20th); Les Misérables (UA–20th); Splendor; The Wedding Night. 1936 Beloved Enemy; Come and Get It; Dodsworth; The Gay Desperado (UA–Pickford Lasky); One Rainy Afternoon (UA–Pickford Lasky); Strike Me Pink; These Three. 1937 Dead End; The Hurricane; Love Under Fire (Fox); A Star Is Born (UA–Selznick); Stella Dallas; Vogues of 1938 (UA–Wanger) w *Irene*; Woman Chases Man. 1938 The Adventures of Marco Polo; The Cowboy and the Lady; The Goldwyn Follies; The Young in Heart (UA–Selznick). 1939 Wuthering Heights.

Muriel King

1936 Sylvia Scarlett (RKO) w *Plunkett, Newman*. 1936 Stage Door (RKO) w *Renie, Newman*. 1941 Back Street (U) w *V West*. 1944 Casanova Brown (RKO–International); Woman in the Window (RKO–International); Christmas Holiday (U) w *V West, Greer*; Cover Girl (Col) w *Wakeling, Banton*.

Norma Koch

1947 The Private Affairs of Bel Ami (UA). 1950 Dakota Lil (Fox). 1951 The Sword of Monte Cristo (Fox). 1952 Rose of Cimarron (Fox). 1954 Apache (UA). 1955 The Kentuckian (UA); Marty (UA); Vera Cruz (UA). 1956 Slightly Scarlet (RKO); While the City Sleeps (RKO). 1957 Sayonara (WB).

1961 Cry for Happy (Col); The Last Sunset (U); Whatever Happened to Baby Jane (WB). 1963 Four for Texas (WB); King of the Sun (UA). 1964 Hush, Hush Sweet Charlotte (Fox). 1967 The Way West (UA).

William Lambert (Fox)

1933 Dangerously Yours; Pleasure Cruise. 1934 Hell in the Heavens; She Was a Lady; The White Parade. 1935 The County Chairman; The Gay Deception; In Old Kentucky; The Little Colonel; Professional Soldier; Redheads on Parade; Thanks a Million; Under Pressure; Way Down East; Welcome Home; One More Spring; Helldorado. 1936 Song and Dance Man; The Country Beyond; Crime of Dr Forbes; Educating Father; Every Saturday Night; The First Baby; Here Comes Trouble; High Tension; Human Cargo.

Mitchell Leisen

1919 Male and Female (Par). 1922 Robin Hood (UA–Fairbanks). 1923 Rosita (UA–Pickford); The Courtship of Miles Standish (Associated Artists). 1924 Dorothy Vernon of Haddon Hall (UA–Pickford); The Thief of Bagdad (UA–Fairbanks). 1932 The Sign of the Cross (Par); 1944 Lady in the Dark (Par) w *Head, Du Bois*. 1949 Bride of Vengeance (Par) w *Grant*.

Charles LeMaire (Fox)

1925 Heart of a Siren (FN). 1929 The Coconuts (Par). 1934 George White's Scandals. 1935 George White's 1935 Scandals. 1941 The Men in Her Life (Col) w *William Bridgehouse*. 1946 Strange Triangle. 1947 Captain From Castile; Kiss of Death. 1948 Escape; Deep Waters; Yellow Sky. 1949 Down to the Sea in Ships; House of Strangers; Pinky; The East Side Story. 1950 All About Eve w *Head*; For Heaven's Sake; My Blue Heaven; Three Came Home; Under My Skin; Wabash Avenue; Halls of Montezuma. 1951 Call Me Mister; Elopement; The Frogmen; Golden Girl; People Will Talk; You're in the Navy Now; I Can Get It for You Wholesale. 1952 The Bloodhounds of Broadway; Five Fingers; My Pal Gus; My Wife's Best Friend; The Snows of Kilimanjaro; With a Song in My Heart; As Young as You Feel. 1953 A Blue Print for Murder; The Desert Rats; Destination Gobi; The Robe w *Santiago*. 1954 Demetrius and the Gladiators; The Egyptian; Prince Valiant; Woman's World. 1955 The Girl in the Red Velvet Swing; Love Is a Many Splendored thing; Soldier of Fortune; The View From Pompey's Head. 1956 The Best Things in Life Are Free; D-Day, the Sixth of June; The Girl Can't Help It; Hilda Crane; The Man in the Grey Flannel Suit. 1957 An Affair to Remember; The Desk Set; Kiss Them for Me; Oh Men! Oh Women!; Stopover Tokyo; The Sun Also Rises; Will Success Spoil Rock Hunter?; Top Secret Affair (WB). 1958 The Barbarian and the Geisha; The Bravados; The Gift of Love; The Hunters; Mardi Gras; A Nice Little Bank That Should Be Robbed; Ten North Frederick. 1959 Compulsion; Rally 'Round the Flag Boys; The Remarkable Mr Pennypacker w *Wills*; Thunder in the Sun (Par); Warlock; The Diary of Anne Frank w *Wills*. 1961 Marriage Go Round. 1962 Walk on the Wild Side (Col).

Don Loper
1948 Ruthless (EL). 1952 Rancho Notorious (RKO). 1953 The Moon Is Blue (U); 1955 The Big Combo (AA); Not as a Stranger (UA–Kramer); Paris Follies of 1956 (AA). 1957 Spring Reunion (UA). 1964 Looking for Love (MGM).

Jean Louis (1944–58 Col; 1959–68 U)
1944 Together Again. 1945 Kiss and Tell; Over 21; A Thousand and One Nights; Tonight and Every Night w *Marcel Vertes*; My Name Is Julia Ross; Voice of the Whistler; The Gay Senorita. 1946 Bandit of Sherwood Forest; Gilda; The Jolson Story; She Wouldn't Say Yes w *Banton*; Tomorrow Is Forever (RKO–International); The Kid From Brooklyn (RKO–Goldwyn) w *White*. 1947 Dead Reckoning; Down to Earth; Blind Spot; Cigarette Girl; The Corpse Came C.O.D.; The Guilt of Janet Ames; It Had To Be You; Johnny O'Clock. 1948 The Black Arrow Strikes; The Dark Past; The Fuller Brush Man; The Gallant Blade; I Love Trouble; The Lady From Shanghai; The Loves of Carmen; You Gotta Stay Happy (U). All the King's Men; Anna Lucasta; Jolson Sings Again; Knock on Any Door; Lust for Gold; Reckless Moment; Shockproof; Tokyo Joe; Undercover Man; The Walking Hills; We Were Strangers. 1950 And Baby Makes Three; Between Midnight and Dawn; Born Yesterday; Cairo to Capetown; Father Is a Bachelor; The Flying Missile; Fortunes of Captain Blood; The Fuller Brush Girl; The Good Humor Man; He's a Cockeyed Wonder; In a Lonely Place; Kill the Umpire; No Sad Songs for Me; The Petty Girl; Rogues of Sherwood Forest; A Woman of Distinction. 1951 The Family Secret; The Magic Carpet; Never Trust a Gambler; Son of Dr Jekyll; The Tall Men. 1952 Affair in Trinidad; Assignment—Paris; The Brigand; The Happy Time; The Marrying Kind; Paula. 1953 Bad for Each Other; The Big Heat; The 5000 Fingers of Dr T; From Here to Eternity; Let's Do It Again; Miss Sadie Thompson Salome w *Santiago*; Serpent of the Nile. 1954 The Caine Mutiny; Human Desire; It Should Happen to You; A Star Is Born (WB) w *Sharaff, Mary Ann Nyberg*. 1955 Count Three and Pray; Five Against the House; The Long Grey Line; My Sister Eileen; Queen Bee; Three for the Show; Tight Spot; The Violent Men. 1956 Autumn Leaves; The Eddy Duchin Story; Jubal; Over-exposed; Picnic; The Solid Gold Cadillac; You Can't Run Away From It. 1957 The Brothers Rico; The Garment Jungle; Jeanne Eagles; Nightfall; Pal Joey; The Story of Esther Costello; The 3:10 to Yuma; The Monte Carlo Story w *Elio Constanzi*. 1958 Bell, Book and Candle. 1959 The Last Angry Man (Col); Imitation of Life; Pillow Talk. 1960 Portrait in Black; Strangers When We Meet (Col); Who Was That Lady? (Col). 1961 Back Street; Judgement at Nuremberg (UA–Kramer). 1962 If a Man Answers. 1963 The Thrill of It All. 1964 Bedtime Story; I'd Rather Be Rich; Send Me No Flowers. 1965 Bus Riley's Back in Town; Mirage; Ship of Fools w *Thomas* (Col); Strange Bedfellows; That Funny Feeling; Madame X. 1966 Blindfold; Gambit; A Man Could Get Killed w *Dimitri Kritsos*. 1966 Banning; Guess Who's Coming to Dinner; Rosie; Thoroughly Modern Millie. 1968 The Ballad of Josie; The Hell With Heroes; P.J. 1972 Lost Horizon (Col). 1973 Forty Carats (Col).

Earl Luick (1928–32 WB; 1933–43 Fox)
1927 Satin Woman (Lumas). 1928 King of Kings (DeM) w *Wakeling*; On Trial. 1929 Conquest; The Desert Song w *Wakeling*; Gold Diggers of Broadway; The Argyle Case; Disraeli; Evidence; General Crack; Honky Tonk; My Man; On With the Show; Queen of the Nightclubs; Sally; Show of Shows; Stark Mad; Stolen Kisses; The Time, the Place and the Girl. 1930 Captain Applejack; The Green Goddess; Hold Everything; The Life of the Party; Little Caesar; The Man From Blankley's; Moby Dick; Oh! Sailor, Behave; Outward Bound; Scarlet Pages; She Couldn't Say No; Sit Tight; Sweet Kitty Bellairs; Three Faces East; Viennese Nights; Old English. 1931 Five Star Final; Expensive Woman; Fifty Million Frenchmen; God's Gift to Women; Gold Dust Gertie; Her Majesty, Love; The Last Flight; The Maltese Falcon; Night Nurse; Public Enemy; Side Show; Svengali. 1932 Woman From Monte Carlo; The Man Who Played God; Hatchet Man; Too Busy to Work (Fox); A Passport to Hell (Fox). 1933 Ever in My Heart (WB); I Loved a Woman (WB); The World Changes (WB); Broadway Bad; Hot Pepper; Cavalcade; The Warrior's Husband; Zoo in Budapest; Pilgrimage. 1942 Footlight Serenade; Springtime in the Rockies; Life Begins at 8:30. 1943 Coney Island w *Rose*; Hello Frisco Hello w *Rose*; Margin for Error.

Moss Mabry (1953–6 WB)
1953 South Seas Woman; Three Sailors and a Girl; Thunder Over the Plains. 1954 The Command; Dial M for Murder; Drumbeat; Lucky Me; The Phantom of the Rue Morgue; Them; The City Is Dark. 1955 Battle Cry; I Died a Thousand Times; Illegal; Rebel Without a Cause; The Sea Chase; Target Zero; Mister Roberts. 1956 The Bad Seed; A Cry in the Night; Giant w *Best*; The Girl He Left Behind; Hell on Frisco Bay; Santiago w *Best*; Toward the Unknown. 1958 Stage Struck (BV). 1960 The Subterraneans (MGM). 1962 The Manchurian Candidate (UA); Mutiny on the Bounty (MGM). 1963 Move Over Darling (Fox); The Ceremony (UA). 1964 Fate Is the Hunter (Fox); Shock Treatment (Fox). 1965 Dear Brigitte (Fox); Harlow (Par) w *Head*; The Reward (Fox). 1966 Murderer's Row (Col); The Silencers (Col); Three on a Couch (Col); Way . . . Way Out! (Fox). 1967 The Big Mouth (Col); A Guide for the Married Man (Fox); Tony Rome (Fox). 1968 The Detective (Fox); How to Save a Marriage and Ruin Your Life (Col); Lady in Cement (Fox); Sol Madrid (MGM); Where Angels Go . . . Trouble Follows (Col). 1969 Bob & Carol & Ted & Alice (Col); The Great Bank Robbery (WB). 1970 R.P.M. (Col); How Do I Love Thee (Cin); The Christine Jorgensen Story (UA). 1974 The Way We Were w *Sharaff* (Col).

Maude Marsh *see* Kathleen Kay

Jay A. Morley Jr (U)
1952 Face to Face (RKO). 1953 The Golden Blade; Walking My Baby Back Home. 1954 Bengal Brigade; Dawn at Socorro; Four Guns to the Border; The Glenn Miller Story; Johnny Dark; Taza, Son of Cochise. 1955 Abbott and Costello Meet the Keystone Cops; The Far Country; The Man From

Bitter Ridge; The Second Greatest Sex; Six Bridges to Cross. 1956 The Creature Walks Among Us; Francis in the Haunted House; The Kettles in the Ozarks; The Mole People; The Price of Fear; Red Sundown; Star in the Dust; There's Always Tomorrow; The Unguarded Moment. 1957 The Deadly Mantis; Guns for a Coward; The Incredible Shrinking Man; Interlude; The Tattered Dress.

Ruth Morley
1958 Never Love a Stranger (AA). 1961 The Hustler (Fox); The Young Doctors (UA). 1962 The Miracle Worker (UA). 1964 Lilith (Col). 1968 The Brotherhood (Par).

Helen A. Myron (Fox)
1935 Charlie Chan in Egypt; My Marriage; Paddy O'Day; This Is the Life; Thunder in the Night. 1936 Charlie Chan's Secret. 1938 The Arizona Wildcat w *Herschel*; Chasing Danger; Checkers; City Girl; Down on the Farm; Mr Moto's Chance; Always in Trouble; Love on a Budget; A Trip to Paris; One Wild Night; Rascals; Safety in Numbers; Speed to Burn; Up the River. 1939 News Is Made at Night; Quick Millions; Everybody's Baby; Boyfriend; Charlie Chan in Honolulu; City of Chance; It Could Happen to You; Mr Moto's Last Warning; Pack up Your Troubles; Stop, Look and Love; Too Busy to Work; Chicken Wagon Family. 1940 Charlie Chan in Panama; Charlie Chan's Murder Cruise; Girl From Avenue A; Lucky Cisco Kid. 1941 Golden Hoofs.

Kay Nelson (Fox)
1944 Up in Mabel's Room (UA); Something for the Boys w *Wood*; Sunday Dinner for a Soldier; Winged Victory. 1945 Diamond Horshoe w *Cashin, R Hubert, LeMaire, Sascha Brastoff*; Leave Her to Heaven. 1946 Behind Green Lights; The Dark Corner; Home Sweet Homicide; Margie; Sentimental Journey; Somewhere in the Night. 1947 Boomerang; Gentleman's Agreement; The Homestretch; Miracle on 34th Street. 1948 Apartment For Peggy; Call Northside 777; Chicken Every Sunday; A Letter to Three Wives; Roadhouse; Sitting Pretty; The Street With No Name; The Walls of Jericho; You Were Meant for Me. 1949 Come to the Stable; Everybody Does It; Father Was a Fullback; Slattery's Hurricane; Mother Is a Freshman; Thieves' Highway. 1954 Witness to Murder (UA). 1955 Daddy Long Legs w *Tom Keogh*; The Racers; Violent Saturday. 1960 Tall Story (WB.)

Bernard Newman (RKO)
1935 Roberta; Break of Hearts; I Dream Too Much; In Person; Star of Midnight; Sylvia Scarlett w *Plunkett, King*; Top Hat. 1936 The Bride Walks Out; The Ex-Mrs Bradord; Follow the Fleet; The Lady Consents; Smartest Girl in Town; Swing Time; Two in the Dark; Walking on Air; The Witness Chair; Theodora Goes Wild. 1937 History is Made at Night (UA–Wanger); When You're in Love (Col). 1938 Vivacious Lady w *Irene*. 1942 Lady in a Jam (U). 1946 Deception (WB). 1947 Dark Passage (WB).

Vittorio Nino Novarese (Fox)
1939 Ettore Fieramosca (Roma); 1860 (Roma). 1949 Black Magic (UA) w *Georges Annenkoff*; Prince of Foxes. 1952 The Thief of Venice. 1954 Crossed Swords (UA). 1955 Shadow of the Eagle (UA). 1960 The Story of Ruth. 1961 Francis of Assisi. 1963 Cleopatra w *Sharaff, Renie*. 1965 The Agony and the Ecstacy; The Greatest Story Ever Told (UA); The War Lord (U). 1967 The King's Pirate (U). 1970 Cromwell (Col).

Mary Ann Nyberg
1953 The Bandwagon (MGM); Lili (MGM). 1954 Carmen Jones (Fox); A Star is Born (WB) w *Sharaff, Louis*.

Sheila O'Brien (WB)
1946 Humoresque w *Adrian*. 1947 Daisy Kenyon (Fox); Possessed. 1950 The Damned Don't Cry; Harriet Craig (Col). 1951 Goodbye My Fancy. 1952 Sudden Fear (RKO); This Woman Is Dangerous. 1954 Johnny Guitar (Rep). 1955 Female on the Beach (U). 1959 The Deadly Companions (AIP). 1965 Never Too Late.

Rosemary Odell (U)
1945 Easy to Look at. 1946 Gunman's Code. 1947 Brute Force; The Wistful Widow of Wagon Gap. 1948 Are You With It?; Feudin', Fussin' and A-Fightin'; Larceny w *Orry Kelly*. 1949 Francis; Free For All; Red Canyon; The Story of Molly X; Yes Sir, That's My Baby; Abbott and Costello Meet the Killer. 1950 I Was a Shoplifter; Louise; Ma and Pa Kettle Go to Town; The Milkman; Outside the Wall; Peggy; Curtain Call at Cactus Creek. 1951 Bedtime For Bonzo; Bright Victory; Comin' Round the Mountain; The Fat Man; Finders Keepers; Francis Goes to the Races; Hollywood Story; Katie Did It; Lady From Texas; Reunion in Reno; The Strange Door. 1952 Battle at Apache Pass; Bend in the River; Has Anybody Seen My Gal?; Here Come the Nelsons; Horizons West; Lawless Breed; Meet Me at the Fair; Sally and Saint Anne; Scarlet Angel. 1953 All I Desire; City Beneath the Sea; Column South; Francis Covers the Big Town; Gunsmoke; It Came From Outer Space; Law and Order; Ma and Pa Kettle on Vacation; Seminole; The Veils of Bagdad; Abbott and Costello Meet Dr Jekyll and Mr Hyde; Thunder Bay. 1954 The Black Shield of Falworth; Border River; Creature From the Black Lagoon; Destry; Ride Clear of Diablo; So This Is Paris; Yankee Pasha. 1955 Abbott and Costello Meet the Mummy; A'in't Misbehavin'; Chief Crazy Horse; Francis in the Navy; Man Without a Star; The Private War of Major Benson; This Island Earth. 1956 Backlash; A Day of Fury; Outside the Law; Pillars of the Sky; Showdown at Abilene; The Square Jungle; Toy Tiger. 1957 Four Girls in Town; Kelly and Me; The Night Runner; Quantez. 1961 Tammy, Tell Me True. 1962 The Spiral Road; To Kill a Mockingbird. 1963 40 Pounds of Trouble; Showdown; Tammy and the Doctor; The Ugly American. 1964 The Brass Bottle; Captain Newman M.D.; The Lively Set; Wild and Wonderful w *Valintino*. 1965 Fluffy; Shenandoah. 1966 The Appaloosa w *Helen Colvig*. 1967 The Ride to Hangman's Tree; Rough Night in Jericho w *Helen Colvig*. 1968 Nobody's Perfect.

Alice O'Neill (UA–Schenck)
1927 The Ladybird (Chadwick). 1928 Drums of Love;

Tempest. 1929 Lady of the Pavements; Married in Hollywood (Fox) w *Wachner*. 1930 The Bad One; Be Yourself!; Just Imagine (Fox) w *Wachner, Tree*; The Lottery Bride; Puttin' on the Ritz; Lummox (UA–Feature Productions).

Adele Palmer (1939–56 Rep; 1957–9 Fox)
1939 Calling All Marines; Should Husbands Work? Smuggled Cargo; The Zero Hour. 1940 Dark Command; Forgotten Girls; Meet the Missus; Money to Burn; Village Barn Dance; Three Faces West; Thou Shalt Not Kill; Wagons Westward; Women in War; Wolf in New York; Who Killed Aunt Maggie?; 1941 Country Fair; The Devil Pays Off; Doctors Don't Tell; The Gay Vagabond; Hurricane Smith; Ice Capades; The Lady From Louisiana; Mercy Island; The Pittsburg Kid; Public Enemies; Rags to Riches; Rookies on Parade; Sailors on Leave; Sis Hopkins. 1942 Flying Tigers; Girl from Alaska; In Old California; Moonlight Masquerade; Pardon My Stripes; Remember Pearl Harbor; Sleepy-time Gal. 1945 Scotland Yard Investigator; Steppin' in Society; Sunset in El Dorado. 1946 The Affairs of Geraldine; Helldorado; The Magnificent Rogue; Man From Rainbow Valley; My Pal Trigger; Night Train to Memphis; One Exciting Week; Rendevous with Auntie; Sioux City Sou; Spectre of The Rose. 1947 Angel and the Badman; Calendar Girl; Driftwood; Exposed; The Fabulous Texan; The Flame; The Ghost Goes Wild; On the Old Spanish Trail; The Pilgrim Lady; Robin Hood of Texas; Saddle Pals; Wyoming. 1948 Angel in Exile; Campus Honeymoon; The Gallant Legion; Grand Canyon Trail; Hearts of Virginia; I, Jane Doe; King of the Gamblers; Lightnin' in the Forest; Moonrise; The Plunderers; Under California Stars; Macbeth; Wake of the Red Witch. 1949 Alias the Champ; Brimstone; Down Dakota Way; Duke of Chicago; Flame of Youth; Hideout; The Kid From Cleveland; Rose of the Yukon; Sands of Iwo Jima; Streets of San Francisco. 1950 Belle of Old Mexico; Harbor of Missing Men; Hit Parade of 1951; The Bull-fighter and the Lady; The Fighting Coast Guard; Pride of Maryland; South of Caliente. 1952 Hoodlum Empire; Oklahoma Annie; The Quiet Man. 1953 Fair Wind to Java; Geraldine; The Woman They Almost Lynched; The Sun Shines Bright. 1954 The Atomic Kid; Jubilee Trail; Make Haste to Live; The Shanghai Story; Untamed Heiress. 1954 The Eternal Sea; The Fighting Chance; The Last Command; The Road to Denver; Santa Fe Passage; Timberjack; The Twinkle in God's Eye. 1956 Come Next Spring; Lisbon; The Maverick Queen; Stranger at My Door; When Gangland Strikes; A Woman's Devotion. 1957 Peyton Place. 1958 In Love and War; The Long Hot Summer; Compulsion. 1959 The Best of Everything; The FBI Story (WB); Hound Dog Man; Say One for Me; The Sound and the Fury.

Walter Plunkett (1926–8 FBO; 1929–40 RKO; 1947–66 MGM)
1926 Ain't Love Funny; One Minute to Play; Red Hot Hoofs; A Regular Scout. 1927 Boy Rider; Clancy's Kosher Wedding; Gingham Girl; Her Summer Hero; Legionnaires in Paris; Lightning Lariats; Magic Garden; Shanghaied. 1928 Bandit's Son; Bantam Cowboy; Captain Careless; Chicago After Midnight; Circus Kid; Headin' For Danger; Hey Rube; Hit of the Show; Phantom on the Range; Sally of the Scandals; Sinners in Love; Son of the Golden West; Stocks and Blondes; Tropic Madness; Wall Flowers; When the Law Rides; Wizard of the Saddle. 1929 Air Legion; Amazing Vagabond; Big Diamond; Robbery; Come and Get It; Dance Hall; Delightful Rogue; Freckled Rascal; Gun Law; Half Marriage; Hardboiled; Hit the Deck; Jazz Age; Laughing at Death; Little Savage; Love Comes Along; Love in the Desert; Night Parade; Outlawed; Pride of the Pawnee; The Red Sword; Rio Rita; 7 Keys to Baldpate; Stolen Love; Street Girl; Syncopation; Tanned Legs; Vagabond Lover; The Very Idea; Voice of the Storm; Queen Kelly; Woman I Love. 1930 Case of Sergeant Grischa; The Cuckoos; Dixiana; Fall Guy; Half Shot at Sunrise; Lawful Larceny; Leathernecking; Love Comes Along; Midnight Mystery; Second Wife. 1931 Cimarron. 1932 The Conquerors; Phantom of Crestwood Secrets of the French Police. 1933 Ace of Aces; Aggie Appleby, Maker of Men; Ann Vickers w *Howard Greer*; Blind Adventure; Chance at Heaven; Christopher String w *Greer*; Crossfire; Emergency Call; Flying Down to Rio w *Irene*; The Great Jasper; Little Women; Lucky Devils; Melody Cruise; Midshipman Jack; Morning Glory w *Greer*; No Marriage Ties; No Other Woman; One Man's Journey; Past of Mary Holmes; Professional Sweetheart; Rafter Romance; Right to Romance; Scarlet River; The Silver Cord; Sweepings; Tomorrow at Seven. 1934 The Age of Innocence; Anne of Green Gables; Bachelor Bait; By Your Leave; Cockeyed Cavaliers; Crime Doctor; Dangerous Corner; Down to Their Last Yacht; Finishing School; The Fountain; The Gay Divorcee; Gridiron Flash; A Hat, a Coat and a Glove; His Greatest Gamble; Keep 'Em Rolling; Kentucky Kernels; The Life of Vergie Winters; The Little Minister; Long Lost Father; Man of Two Worlds; Meanest Gal in Town; Of Human Bondage; Romance in Manhattan; The Silver Streak; Sing and Like It; Spifire; Stingaree; Success at Any Price; Their Big Moment; This Man Is Mine; Wednesday's Child; We're Rich Again; Woman in the Dark. 1935 Alice Adams; Annie Oakley; Another Face; The Arizonian; Captain Hurricane; Chasing Yesterday; A Dog of Flanders; Enchanted April; Freckles; Grand Old Girl; His Family Tree; Hooray For Love; Hot Tip; The Informer; Jalna; Lightening Strikes Twice; Murder on a Honeymoon; The Return of Peter Grimm; Seven Keys to Baldpate; Strangers All; Sylvia Scarlett w *Newman, King*; The Three Musketeers; Village Tale. 1936 Chatterbox; Mary of Scotland; The Plough and the Stars; A Woman Rebels. 1937 Nothing Sacred (UA–Selznick) w *Banton*; Quality Street; The Soldier and the Lady; The Woman I Love. 1938 The Adventures of Tom Sawyer (UA–Selznick). 1939 The Story of Vernon and Irene Castle; Stagecoach (UA-Wanger); The Hunchback of Notre Dame; Gone With the Wind (MGM–Selznick). 1940 Abe Lincoln in Illinois; Captain Caution (UA); Vigil in the Night. 1941 The Corsican Brothers (UA); Go West Young Lady (Col); Ladies in Retirement (Col); Lady for a Night (Rep); Lydia (UA–Korda) w *Marcel Vertes*; Sundown (UA). 1942 To Be or Not to Be (UA) w *Irene*. 1943 The Commandoes Strike at Dawn (Col); The Heat's On (Col). 1944 Can't Help Singing (U);

Knickerbocker Holiday (UA). 1945 Along Came Jones (RKO–International); A Song to Remember (Col) w *Banton*. 1946 Because of Him (U) w *V West*; Duel in the Sun (UA–Selznick); My Brother Talks to Horses. 1947 Fiesta w *Irene*; Green Dolphin Street w *Valles*; Sea of Grass; Song of Love. 1948 The Kissing Bandit; Summer Holiday; The Three Muskateers. 1949 Adam's Rib; Little Women; Madame Bovary w *Valles*; The Secret Garden; Ambush; That Forsythe Woman. 1950 Annie Get Your Gun w *Rose*; The Black Hand; Father of the Bride w *Rose*; King Solomon's Mines; The Magnificent Yankee; Ths Miniver Story; The Outriders; Stars in My Crown; Summer Stock w *Rose*; The Happy Years The Toast of New Orleans w *Rose*. 1951 Across the Wide Missouri; An American in Paris w *Sharaff, Orry Kelly*; Kind Lady w *Steele*; The Law and the Lady; Man with a Cloak; Mr Imperium; Showboat; Soldiers Three; Vengeance Valley; Westward the Women. 1952 Million Dollar Mermaid w *Rose*; Plymouth Adventure; The Prisoner of Zenda; Singin' in the Rain. 1953 The Actress; All the Brothers Were Valiant; Kiss Me Kate; Ride, Vaquero; Young Bess; Scandal at Scourie. 1954 7 Brides for 7 Brothers; Athena; The Student Prince w *Rose*; Valley of the Kings. 1955 Deep in My Heart w *Rose*; The Glass Slipper w *Rose*; Jupiter's Darling w *Rose*; The King's Thief; Many Rivers to Cross; Moonfleet; The Scarlet Coat; Tribute to a Badman. 1956 Diane; The Fastest Gun Alive; Forbidden Planet w *Rose*; Lust For Life. 1957 Gun Glory; Raintree County; The Wings of Eagles. 1958 The Brothers Karamazov; The Law and Jake Wade; Merry Andrew; The Sheepman; Some Came Running. 1959 Home From the Hill. 1960 Bells Are Ringing; Pollyanna (Disney). 1961 Cimarron; Pocketful of Miracles (UA) w *Head*. 1962 The Four Horsemen of the Apocalypse w *R Hubert, Orry Kelly*; How the West Was Won. 1965 Marriage on the Rocks (WB). 1966 Seven Women.

Natacha Rambova
1921 Forbidden Fruit (Par) w *Leisen*; Camille (MGM); Salome (Nazimova).

Max Ree (1926 MGM; 1927–9 FN; 1930–2 RKO)
1926 The Scarlet Letter; The Temptress with *Andre-Ani, Marsh, Kay*; The Torrent w *Andre-Ani, Marsh, Kay*. 1927 The Private Life of Helen of Troy; The Wedding March (Par); The Love Mart; Rose of the Golden West; The Stolen Bride. 1928 The Divine Lady; The Barker; Show Girl; The Yellow Lily. 1929 Broadway Babies; Hot Stuff; The Man and the Moment; Weary River; Side Street (RKO). 1930 Conspiracy; The Royal Bed; She's My Weakness; Inside the Line; Shooting Straight; The Silver Hoard; The Sin Ship; Hook, Line, and Sinker. 1931 Are These Our Children?; Cracked Nuts; The Lady Refuses; Girl of the Rio; Transgression; Travelling Husbands; Bachelor Apartment; Behind Office Doors; Men of Chance; Secret Service; Smart Woman; High Stakes; Fanny Foley Herself; The Public Defender; White Shoulders; The Woman Between; Kept Husbands. 1932 Ladies of the Jury. 1935 A Midsummer Night's Dream (WB) w *Anderson*. 1947 Carnegie Hall (UA–LeBaron).

Renie (1937–57 Fox)
1937 Stage Door w *King*; High Flyers; Saturday's Heroes; Forty Naughty Girls; Quick Money; Everybody's Doing It; Night Spot. 1938 Mr Doodle Kicks Off; Next Time I Marry; Crime Ring; Double Danger; The Affairs of Annabel; I'm From the City; Having a Wonderful Time w *Stevenson*; Fugitives For a Night; Law of the Underworld; Twelve Crowded Hours; Tarnished Angel. 1939 The Girl and the Gambler; The Girl From Mexico; Go Chase Yourself; The Rookie Cop; The Saint Strikes Back; The Saint Takes Over; The Saint's Double Trouble; Almost a Gentleman; Sued for Libel; Two Thoroughbreds; Conspiracy; The Day the Bookies Wept; Career; Married and in Love. 1940 The Marines Fly High; Men Against the Sky; Mexican Spitfire Out West; Millionaire Playboy; Millionaire in Prison; Bill of Divorcement; Curtain Call; Stranger on the Third Floor; Kitty Foyle; The Saint in Palm Springs; Lucky Partners w *Irene*; The Tuttles of Tahiti; The Great Man Votes; One Crowded Night; The Primrose Path. 1941 Call Out the Marines; A Date With the Falcon; Unexpected Uncle; Sing Your Worries Away; Tom, Dick and Harry; The Gay Falcon; Lady Scarface; Footlight Fever; Four Jacks and a Jill; Obliging Young Lady; Repent at Leisure; Parachute Batallion; The Falcon Takes Over. 1942 Forever and a Day w *Plunkett, Stevenson*; Here We Go Again; Hitler's Children; The Big Street; Seven Days Leave; The Tuttles of Tahiti; Cat People; The Mayor of 44th Street; Mexican Spitfire Sees a Ghost; Mexican Spitfire's Baby; Mexican Spitfire's Elephant; The Navy Comes Through; The Falcon's Brother. 1943 Mexican Spitfire's Blessed Event; The Seventh Victim; The Sky's the Limit; Tender Comrade w *Head*; This Land Is Mine; The Falcon and the Co-eds; The Falcon in Danger; The Falcon Out West; The Falcon Strikes Back; Rookies in Burma; Mr Lucky; Petticoat Larceny. 1944 Days of Glory; Music in Manhattan; My Pal, Wolf; A Night of Adventure; Pan-Americana; Passport to Destiny; None But the Lonely Heart; The Falcon in Hollywood; The Falcon in Mexico: Heavenly Days; Girl Rush; Two O'Clock Courage; The Brighton Strangler. 1945 Wander of the Wasteland; Back to Bataan; Those Endearing Young Charms; A Game of Death; Genius at Work; West of the Pecos; Deadline at Dawn; 1946 A Likely Story; Badman's Journey; The Bamboo Blonde; Step by Step; Crack-up. 1947 Station West; The Long Night; If You Knew Susie; Riff-raff; The Miracle of the Bells. 1951 As Young as You Feel; Follow the Sun; The Guy Who Came Back; House on Telegraph Hill; Let's Make It Legal; Love Nest; The Model and the Marriage Broker; Mr Belvedere Rings the Bell. 1952 We're Not Married; Night Without Sleep; Return of the Texan; Wait Till the Sun Shines Nellie. 1953 Dangerous Crossing; The I Don't Care Girl; Mr Scoutmaster; The President's Lady; Vicki; Taxi. 1954 The Siege at Red River. 1955 A Man Called Peter. 1956 The King and Four Queens (UA). 1957 April Love; The Three Faces of Eve. 1958 The Girl Most Likely (RKO). 1959 The Big Fisherman (BV). 1961 Snow White and the Three Stooges (Fox). 1963 Cleopatra (Fox) w *Sharaff, Novarese*. 1964 Circus World (Par); The Pleasure Seekers (Fox). 1966 The Sand Pebbles (Fox). 1968 The Killing of Sister George (Cin); The Legend of

Lylah Clare (MGM). 1969 Whatever Happened to Aunt Alice? (Cin).

Leah Rhodes (WB)

1943 Old Acquaintance w *Orry Kelly*; Mission to Moscow; Northern Pursuit. 1944 Passage to Marseilles; Between Two Worlds; Janie; The Conspirators; Experiment Perilous (RKO) w *Stevenson*. 1945 Roughly Speaking; God Is My Co-Pilot; Hotel Berlin; Confidential Agent; Too Young to Know. 1946 My Reputation w *Head*; Saratoga Trunk; Her Kind of Man; Janie Gets Married; Two Guys From Milwaukee; The Big Sleep; Cloak and Dagger; Never Say Goodbye; Night Unto Night. 1947 Pursued; Stallion Road; That Hagen Girl. 1948 Always Leave Them Laughing; My Girl Tisa; Voice of the Turtle; Winter Meeting w *Head*; Wallflower; Key Largo; Two Guys From Texas; June Bride w *Head*. 1949 The Adventures of Don Juan w *Travilla, Best*; Colorado Territory; The Girl From Jones Beach; White Heat; Task Force; The Story of Seabiscuit. 1950 Backfire; Chained Lightning; Caged; Tea for Two; Bright Leaf; The Breaking Point; Three Secrets. 1951 Only the Valiant; Strangers on a Train; Mark of the Renegade (U); The Golden Horde (U); Come Fill the Cup; Starlift. 1952 Room for One More; I'll See You in My Dreams; Bugles in the Afternoon; About Face; The Winning Team; 1953 April in Paris; By the Light of the Silvery Moon; So This Is Love. 1957 Forty Guns (Fox). 1958 Kings Go Forth. 1965 Tickle Me (AA); Village of the Giants (Emb). 1966 Picture Mommy Dead (Emb). 1967 Good Times (Col). 1968 The Fox (WB); Five Card Stud (Par).

Helen Rose (MGM)

1943 Coney Island (Fox) w *Luick*; Hello Frisco, Hello (Fox) w *Luick*; Stormy Weather. 1946 The Harvey Girls w *Valles*; Two Sisters From Boston w *Valles*; Ziegfeld Follies w *Sharaff*; Till the Clouds Roll By w *Valles*. 1947 Good News w *Valles*; Merton of the Movies w *Valles*; The Unfinished Dance. 1948 Act of Violence; A Date With Judy; Homecoming; Words and Music w *Valles*; Luxury Liner w *Valles*; The Bride Goes Wild. 1949 On the Town; The Red Danube; The Stratton Story; Take Me Out to the Ballgame w *Valles*; East Side, West Side. 1950 A Life of Her Own; Pagan Love Song; Summer Stock w *Plunkett*; Three Little Words; To Please a Lady; The Toast of New Orleans w *Plunkett*; The Reformer and the Redhead; Annie Get Your Gun w *Plunkett*; Father of the Bride w *Plunkett*; The Duchess of Idaho; The Big Hangover; Grounds for Marriage. 1951 Father's Little Dividend; The Great Caruso w *Steele*; The Light Touch; Texas Carnival; The Unknown Man; Excuse My Dust w *Steele*; No Questions Asked; Strictly Dishonorable; The Strip; Too Young to Kiss; Callaway Went Thataway; The People Against O'Hara w *Steele*; Love Is Better Than Ever. 1952 The Girl in White w *Steele*; Above and Beyond; The Bad and the Beautiful; Because You're Mine; Everything I Have Is Yours; Glory Alley; Holiday for Sinners; Invitation; The Merry Widow w *Steele*; Million Dollar Mermaid w *Plunkett*; Shirts Ahoy!, The Belle of New York w *Steele*; Washington Story. 1953 Dangerous When Wet; Dream Wife w *Herschel*; Jeopardy; Latin Lovers w *Herschel*; Mogambo; Sombrero; The Story of Three Loves; Torch Song; I Love Melvin; Small Town Girl; Remains to Be Seen; Easy to Love. 1954 Athena w *Plunkett*; Executive Suite; Green Fire; Her Twelve Men; The Last Time I Saw Paris; The Long, Long Trailer; Rhapsody; Rogue Cop; Rose Marie w *Plunkett*; The Student Prince w *Plunkett*; The Glass Slipper w *Plunkett*. 1955 Bedevilled w *Jean Desses*; Deep in My Heart w *Plunkett*; Hit the Deck; I'll Cry Tomorrow; Interrupted Melody; It's Always Fair Weather; Jupiter's Darling w *Plunkett*; Love Me or Leave Me; The Rains of Ranchipur (Fox) w *Travilla*; The Tender Trap. 1956 Forbidden Planet w *Plunkett*; Gaby; High Society; Meet Me in Las Vegas; The Opposite Sex; The Power and the Prize; Ransom!; The Swan; Tea and Sympathy; These Wilder Years. 1957 Designing Woman; Don't Go Near the Water; The Seventh Sin; Silk Stockings; Something of Value; Tip on a Dead Jockey; Ten Thousand Bedrooms. 1958 Cat on a Hot Tin Roof; The High Cost of Loving; Party Girl; The Reluctant Debutante w *Pirrre Balmain*; Saddle the Wind; The Tunnel of Love; The High Cost of Loving. 1959 Ask Any Girl; Count Your Blessings; It Started With a Kiss; The Mating Game. 1960 All the Fine Young Cannibals; Butterfield 8; The Gazebo; Never So Few. 1961 Ada; Bachelor in Paradise; Go Naked in the World; The Honeymoon Machine. 1963 The Courtship of Eddie's Father. 1964 Goodbye Charlie (Fox). 1966 Made in Paris; Mister Buddwing.

Royer (1933–9 Fox)

1933 The Masquerader (UA–Goldwyn); Charlie Chan's Greatest Case; The Last Trail; Life in the Raw; The Mad Game; Olsen's Big Moment; Smoky; Walls of Gold; It's Great to be Alive; Jimmy and Sally. 1934 Baby Take a Bow; Bright Eyes; Such Women Are Dangerous; Orient Express; I Believed in You; Hold That Girl; Wild Gold; 365 Nights in Hollywood; Three on a Honeymoon; Pursued; Murder in Trinidad; Love Time; Handy Andy; Charlie Chan's Courage; Charlie Chan in London. 1935 Beauty's Daughter; Black Sheep; Great Hotel Murder; Ladies Love Danger; Mystery Woman; Charlie Chan in Shanghai; Charlie Chan's Secret; Dante's Inferno; Hard Rock Harrigan. 1936 Lloyds of London; One in a Million; Sing Baby Sing; Sins of Man; To Mary with Love. 1937 Cafe Metropole; Fifty Roads to Town; Love and Hisses; Love Is News; Slave Ship; Thin Ice; This Is My Affair; You Can't Have Everything. 1938 Always Goodbye; Four Men and a Prayer; Happy Landing; Hold That Co-ed; In Old Chicago; Suez; Josette; Kentucky Moonshine; My Lucky Star. 1939 Jesse James; Rose of Washington Square; Stanley and Livingstone; Swanee River; The Three Musketeers; Young Mr Lincoln; Daytime Wife; Second Fiddle. 1940 Turnabout (UA–Roach). 1941 Model Wife (U) w *V. West*; The Shanghai Gesture (UA) w *Cassini*. 1942 Friendly Enemies (UA); Miss Annie Rooney (UA–Small); About Face (UA).

Theadora Van Runkle (WB)

1967 Bonnie and Clyde. 1968 Bullitt; I Love You Alice B. Toklas; The Thomas Crown Affair (UA). 1969 The Reivers. 1974 Mame; The Godfather Part 2 (Par).

Irene Saltern (Rep)

1938 Army Girl; Call of the Yukon; Gangs of New York; King of the Newsboys; The Night Hawk; Romance on the Run; Storm over Bengal; Under Western Stars. 1939 Federal Man-hunt; Forged Passport; The Mysterious Miss X; Pride of the Navy; Woman Doctor. 1940 Miracle on Main Street (Col); The Howards of Virginia (Col); The Westerner (UA). 1941 All-American Co-ed w *Travilla*; Miss Polly; So Ends Our Night; Cheers for Miss Bishop; They Dare Not Love (Col).

Emile Santiago

1952 Androcles and the Lion (RKO). 1953 The Robe (Fox) w *LeMaire*; Salome (Col) w *Louis*. 1955 Strange Lady in Town (WB). 1958 The Big Country (UA) w *Wood*.

Irene Sharaff (1943–5 MGM)

1943 Girl Crazy; I Dood It w *Steele*; Madame Curie w *Steele*. 1944 Meet Me in St Louis. 1945 Yolanda and the Thief w *Irene*. 1946 The Best Years of Our Lives (RKO–Goldwyn); The Dark Mirror (U); Zeigfeld Follies (MGM) w *Rose*. 1947 The Bishop's Wife (RKO–Goldwyn); The Secret Life of Walter Mitty (RKO–Goldwyn). 1948 Every Girl Should Be Married (RKO); A Song Is Born (RKO–Goldwyn). 1951 An American in Paris (MGM) w *Plunkett, Orry Kelly*. 1953 Call Me Madam (Fox). 1954 Brigadoon (MGM); A Star Is Born (WB) w *Louis, Mary Ann Nyberg*. 1955 Guys and Dolls (MGM–Goldwyn). 1956 The King and I (Fox). 1959 Porgy and Bess (Col–Goldwyn). 1960 Can-Can (Fox) w *Tony Duquette*. 1961 Flower Drum Song (U); West Side Story (UA). 1963 Cleopatra (Fox) w *Renie, Novarese*. 1965 The Sandpiper (MGM). 1966 Who's Afraid of Virginia Woolf? (WB). 1967 The Taming of the Shrew (Col) w *Danilo Donati*. 1968 Funny Girl (Col). 1969 Justine (Fox); Hello Dolly (Fox). 1970 The Great White Hope (Fox). 1974 The Way We Were (Col) w *Mabry*.

Howard Shoup (1937–40 WB; 1942–6 MGM)

1937 Expensive Husbands; The Footloose Heiress; Her Husband's Secretary; Love Is on the Air; Over the Goal; The Perfect Specimen; Ready Willing and Able; San Quentin; Submarine D-1; Varsity Show. 1938 Alcatraz Island; Boy Meets Girl; Broadway Musketeers; Garden of the Moon; Gold Diggers in Paris; Love Honor and Behave; Men Are Such Fools; Four Daughters w *Orry Kelly*; Nancy Drew, Detective; Racket Busters; A Slight Case of Murder; Swing Your Lady. 1939 Each Dawn I Die; Espionage Agent; Four Wives; On Trial; Yes, My Darling Daughter; Nine Lives Are Not Enough; Daughters Courageous. 1940 Brother Orchid; It All Came True; The Story of Dr Ehrlich's Magic Bullet; Torrid Zone. 1942 All Through the Night (WB); Captain of the Clouds (WB); Nazi Agent; Born to Sing; A Yank on the Burma Road; Seven Sweethearts; Jackass Mail; Tarzan's New York Adventure; Grand Central Murder; Once Upon a Thursday; Whistling in Dixie; Northwest Rangers. 1943 The Youngest Profession; Assignment in Brittany w *Steele*; Dubarry Was a Lady w *Steele*; A Stranger in Town. 1946 Little Mr Jim; The Mighty McGirk; The Showoff. 1952 Stop,

You're Killing Me. 1953 Calamity Jane; The Eddie Cantor Story w *Best*; House of Wax; The Jazz Singer; She's Back on Broadway. 1954 The Will Rogers Story; The Young at Heart. 1955 The Court Martial of Billy Mitchell; The McConnell Story; Pete Kelly's Blues; Sincerely Yours. 1956 Bundle of Joy (RKO); Serenade. 1957 Bombers B-52; The Helen Morgan Story; The Unholy Wife (RKO). 1958 The Deep Six; Home Before Dark; I Married a Woman (RKO); Island of Lost Women; Marjorie Morningstar; Onionhead. 1959 A Summer Place; Westbound; The Young Philadelphians. 1960 The Bramble Bush; Cash McCall; The Crowded Sky; Ice Palace; Oceans Eleven; The Rise and Fall of Legs Diamond. 1961 Claudelle Inglish; A Fever in the Blood; Parrish; Portrait of a Mobster; Susan Slade. 1962 Rome Adventure. 1963 Wall of Noise. 1964 A Distant Trumpet; Kisses for My President; Youngblood Hawke. 1965 A Rage to Live. 1966 An American Dream. 1967 Cool Hand Luke; The Cool Ones; Hotel w *Head*. 1969 If It's Tuesday, This Must Be Belgium (UA).

Gile Steele (MGM)

1938 The Toy Wife w *Adrian*; Yellow Jack; Marie Antoinette w *Adrian*. 1940 Bittersweet w *Adrian*; Boomtown w *Adrian*; Edison the Man w *Tree*; Escape w *Adrian*; Go West w *Tree*; The Mortal Storm w *Adrian*; New Moon w *Adrian*; Strike Up the Band w *Tree*; Waterloo Bridge w *Adrian*; Little Nelly Kelly w *Tree*; Pride and Prejudice w *Adrian*; A Yank at Eton w *Shoup*; Wyoming w *Tree*; Comrade X w *Adrian*; Florian w *Adrian*. 1941 Blossoms in the Dust w *Adrian*; Dr Jekyll and Mr Hyde w *Adrian*; A Woman's Face w *Adrian*; The Chocolate Soldier w *Adrian*; Billy the Kid w *Tree*; Bad Man w *Tree*; Honky Tonk w *Kalloch*; Smilin' Through w *Adrian*; They Met in Bombay w *Adrian*; The Bugle Sounds w *Kalloch*; H.M. Pulham Esquire w *Kalloch*. 1942 Mrs Miniver w *Kalloch*; Born to Sing; Pierre of the Plains w *Shoup*; Jackass Mail w *Shoup*; Rio Rita w *Kalloch*; Tortilla Flat w *Kalloch*; For Me and My Gal w *Kalloch*. 1943 I Dood It w *Sharaff*; Madame Curie w *Sharaff*; Best Foot Forward w *Irene*; The Man From Down Under w *Shoup*; Assignment in Brittany w *Shoup*; Above Suspicion w *Irene*; Dubarry Was a Lady w *Shoup*; The Cross of Lorraine; Song of Russia w *Irene*. 1944 The White Cliffs of Dover w *Irene*; Meet the People w *Irene*. 1946 Monsieur Beaucaire (Par) w *Dodson*. 1948 The Emperor Waltz (Par) w *Head*; I Remember Mama (RKO) w *Stevenson*. 1949 A Connecticut Yankee in King Arthur's Court (Par) w *Dodson*; The Heiress (Par) w *Head*; Samson and Delilah (Par) w *Head, Jeakins, Wakeling, Elois Jenssen*. 1950 Fancy Pants (Par) w *Head*. 1951 The Great Caruso w *Rose*; Kind Lady w *Plunkett*; Excuse My Dust w *Rose*; Callaway Went Thataway w *Rose*; The People Against O'Hara w *Rose*. 1952 Lone Star; The Merry Widow w *Rose*; Scaramouche.

Edward Stevenson (1929 FN; 1930–1 WB; 1936–49 RKO; 1950–3 Fox)

1929 Footlights and Fools; Smiling Irish Eyes; Sally. 1930 Kismet; Sunny; Song of the Flame; Peacock Alley (Tiffany); Mamba (Tiffany). 1931 Alexander Hamilton; Five Star Final; Bright Lights. 1933 The Bitter Tea of General Yen (Col).

1936 Grand Jury; Mummy's Boys; The Plot Thickens; Second Wife; That Girl From Paris; They Wanted to Marry; Wanted—Jane Turner; We're on the Jury. 1937 You Can't Beat Love; You Can't Buy Luck; Too Many Wifes; There Goes My Girl; There Goes the Groom; The Toast of New York; Super Sleuth; She's Got Everything; Sea Devils; Music for Madame; New Faces of 1937; Out of the Past; Hitting a New High; The Life of the Party; Don't Tell Your Wife; Breakfast for Two. 1938 Blonde Cheat; Having a Wonderful Time w Renie; Joy of Living w Kalloch; Maid's Night Out; Mother Carey's Chickens; Pacific Liner; Radio City Revels; The Saint in New York; Smashlng the Rackets; This Marriage Business. 1939 They Made Her a Spy; Three Sons; Sorority House; Reno; Panama Lady; Nurse Edith Cavell; Five Came Back; In Name Only w Irene; Gunga Din; Love Affair w Greer; Beauty for the Asking; That's Right, You're Wrong. 1940 Dance Girl Dance; Anne of Windy Poplars; Let's Make Music; No, No, Nanette; Swiss Family Robinson; They Knew What They Wanted; Tom Brown's Schooldays; Too Many Girls; You Can't Fool Your Wife; You'll Find Out; Irene. 1941 Weekend for Three; Valley of the Sun; They Met in Argentina; Suspicion; Playmates; My Life with Caroline; Mexican Spitfire at Sea; Joan of Paris; A Girl, a Guy, and a Gob; Look Who's Laughing; Citizen Kane. 1942 Forever and a Day w Plunkett, Renie; My Favorite Spy; Syncopation; The Magnificent Ambersons; The Fallen Sparrow; The Iron Major; A Lady Takes a Chance; Higher and Higher; The Curse of the Cat People; Government Girl. 1944 Step Lively; Show Business; What a Blonde; Having a Wonderful Crime; China Sky; Passport to Destiny; Youth Runs Wild; Zombies on Broadway; Murder My Sweet; Marine Raiders. 1945 Man Alive; The Enchanted Cottage; Experiment Perilous w Rhodes; Bedlam; George White's Scandals; From This Day Forward; The Truth About Murder; The Spiral Staircase; The Spanish Main. 1946 They Won't Believe Me; Sinbad the Sailor; The Bachelor and the Bobby Soxer; Do You Love Me (Fox). 1947 It's a Wonderful Life; Race Street; Woman on the Beach. 1948 I Remember Mama w Steele; A Woman's Secret; Blood on the Moon; The Judge Steps Out. 1949 Easy Living. 1950 Walk Softly (RKO); Cheaper by the Dozen; The Jackpot; The Mudlark w Furse; Stella (RKO); Two Flags West. 1951 Anne of the Indies; David and Bathsheba; The Desert Fox; Fourteen Hours; I'd Climb the Highest Mountain; The Secret of Convict Lake; The Thirteenth Letter. 1952 Kangaroo; O'Henry's Full House; Red Skies of Montana; What Price Glory; Against All Flags (U); The Redhead From Wyoming (U); At Sword's Point. 1953 The Silver Whip (Fox); War Arrow (U). 1954 Lady Godiva (U). 1956 The First Treveling Saleslady (RKO). 1960 The Facts of Life w Head.

Anthea Sylbert
1968 Rosemary's Baby. 1974 Chinatown; 1975 Shampoo.

Helen Taylor (1936 Par; 1937–8 UA–Wanger)
1935 The Melody Lingers On (UA–Reliance). 1936 Big Brown Eyes; The Case Against Mrs Ames; Fatal Lady; The Moon's Our Home; Palm Springs; Spendthrift; The Trail of the Lonesome Pine. 1937 Stand-In; You Only Live Once. 1938 I Met My Love Again; Trade Winds w Irene.

Bill Thomas (1950–60 U; 1961–74 BV)
1950 Undercover Girl; Saddle Tramp; The Desert Hawk; Kansas Raiders; Mystery Submarine. 1951 Apache Drums; Cave of Outlaws; The Cimarron Kid; Thunder on the Hill; Tomahawk; Flame of Araby; The Iron Man; The Lady Pays Off; The Prince Who Was a Thief; The Raging Tide; Smuggler's Island; Weekend With Father. 1952 Because of You; The Black Castle; Bonzo Goes to College; Bronco Buster; The World in His Arms; Little Egypt; Flesh and Fury; Meet Dany Wilson; No Room for the Groom; The Raiders; Steel Town; Untamed Frontier; Yankee Buccaneer. 1953 Back to God's Country; The Mississippi Gambler; East of Sumatra; Desert Legion; Forbidden; The Glass Web; It Happens Every Thursday; The Man From the Alamo; The Stand at Apache River; Wings of the Hawk; Take Me to Town. 1954 Black Horse Canyon; Magnificent Obsession; Saskatchewan; Playgirl; Rails into Laramie; The Yellow Mountain. 1955 Captain Lightfoot; Foxfire; One Desire; The Purple Mask; Running Wild; Sign of the Pagan; Smoke Signal. 1956 All that Heaven Allows; Behind the High Wall; The Benny Goodman Story; Congo Crossing; I've Lived Before; Never Say Goodbye; Raw Edge; The Rawhide Years; The Spoilers; Walk the Proud Land; World in My Corner. 1957 Battle Hymn; The Girl in the Kremlin; The Great Man; Istanbul; Man Afraid; Man of a Thousand Faces w Marilyn Sotto; The Midnight Story; Floodtide; Mister Cory; My Man Godfrey; Night Passage; Rock, Pretty Baby; Slaughter on Tenth Avenue; Slim Carter; Tammy and the Bachelor; Written on the Wind. 1958 Appointment With a Shadow; Day of the Bad Man; The Female Animal; Kathy O; The Lady Takes a Flyer; Live Fast, Die Young; Man in the Shadow; Monster on the Campus; Once Upon a Horse; The Restless Years; Ride a Crooked Mile; The Saga of Hemp Brown; Summer Love; The Tarnished Angels; The Thing That Couldn't Die; This Happy Feeling; A Time to Love and a Time to Die; Touch of Evil; Twilight for the Gods. 1959 Beloved Infidel; Curse of the Undead; Operation Petticoat; The Rabbit Trap; Step Down to Terror; Stranger in my Arms; Take a Giant Step; This Earth Is Mine. 1960 Spartacus w Valles; The Leech Woman; High Time (Fox); North to Alaska (Fox); One Foot in Hell (Fox); Seven Thieves (Fox); Wake Me When It's Over (Fox). 1961 Babes in Toyland; By Love Possessed (UA); The Parent Trap; Romanoff and Juliet (Ustinov). 1962 Bon Voyage; Moon Pilot. 1963 The Prize (MGM); Son of Flubber; Summer Magic; Toys in the Attic (UA). 1964 The Americanization of Emily (MGM); Honeymoon Hotel (MGM); Kiss Me, Stupid (UA); Mary Poppins w Tony Walton. 1965 Cat Ballou (Col); Inside Daisy Clover (WB) w Head; Ship of Fools (Col) w Louis; That Darn Cat. 1966 Follow Me, Boys; Lt Robinson Crusoe U.S.N. 1967 The Adventures of Bullwhip Griffin; The Gnome-Mobile; The Happiest Millionaire; Monkeys Go Home. 1968 Blackbeard's Ghost; The Horse in the Gray Flannel Suit; The Love Bug; Never a Dull Moment; The One and Only Genuine Family Band. 1969 The Trouble With Girls (MGM); The Undefeated

(Fox). 1970 The Hawaiians (UA). 1971 Bedknobs and Broomsticks. 1974 The Island at the Top of the World. 1975 Logan's Run (MGM).

William Travilla (1941–3 Col; 1946–9 WB; 1950–68 Fox) 1941 All-American Co-ed w *Saltern*. 1943 The Desperadoes; Redhead From Manhattan. 1946 Night and Day w *Anderson*. 1947 Always Together; My Wild Irish Rose; The Unfaithful. 1948 The Adventures of Don Juan w *Best, Rhodes*; Good Sam (RKO); Silver River. 1949 Flamingo Road w *O'Brien*; Look for the Silver Lining; Inspector General; Dancing in the Dark (Fox). 1950 An American Guerrilla in the Phillipines; The Gunfighter; I'll Get By; Mister 880; Mother Didn't Tell Me; No Way Out; Panic in the Streets; When Willie Comes Marching Home; Woman on the Run (U). 1951 Bird of Paradise; The Day the Earth Stood Still; Half Angel; Meet Me After the Show; On the Riviera w *Cassini*; Rawhide; Take Care of My Little Girl. 1952 Don't Bother to Knock; Dreamboat; Lydia Bailey; Monkey Business; The Pride of St Louis; She's Working Her Way Through College (WB) w *Best*; Viva Zapata. 1953 Down Among the Sheltering Palms; The Farmer Takes a Wife; Gentlemen Prefer Blondes; The Girl Next Door; How to Marry a Millionaire; King of the Khyber Rifles; Man in the Attic; Pickup on South Street; Powder River; 1954 Black Widow; Broken Lance; The Gambler from Natchez; Garden of Evil; Hell and High Water; The Raid; River of No Return; The Rocket Man; Three Young Texans. 1955 Gentlemen Marry Brunettes (UA); How to Be Very, Very Popular; The Rains of Ranchipur w *Rose*; The Seven Year Itch; The Tall Men; There's No Business Like Show Business w *White*; White Feather. 1956 The Bottom of the Bottle; Bus Stop; The Lieutenant Wore Skirts; The Proud Ones; The Revolt of Mamie Stover; 23 Paces to Baker Street. 1957 The Fuzzy Pink Nightgown (UA). 1960 From the Terrace. 1963 Mary, Mary (WB); The Stripper; Take Her She's Mine. 1965 Signpost to Murder (MGM). 1967 Valley of the Dolls. 1968 The Boston Strangler; The Secret Life of an American Wife. 1969 Daddy's Gone A-Hunting (WB). 1970 WUSA (Par). 1971 The Big Cube (WB).

Dolly Tree (MGM) 1931 Bad Girl (Fox). 1933 Beauty for Sale; Meet the Baron; The Prizefighter and the Lady. 1934 Evelyn Prentice; The Gay Bride; Hide-Out; Manhattan Melodrama; Stamboul Quest; Straight Is the Way; West Point of the Air; Laughing Boy; Woman Wanted; You Can't Buy Everything; A Wicked Woman; Viva Villa; The Thin Man. 1935 Age of Indiscretion; Ah, Wilderness; The Casino Murder Case; David Copperfield; A Night at the Opera; The Night Is Young; Public Hero No. 1; A Tale of Two Cities; Times Square Lady; Vanessa— Her Love Story; The Flame Within; Escapade; The Bishop Misbehaves; The Perfect Gentleman; Riffraff; It's in the Air. 1936 Exclusive Story; After the Thin Man; Fury; Mad Holiday; Libeled Lady; Small Town Girl; Suzy; Wife Versus Secretary; The Unguarded Hour; Moonlight Murder; Picaddilly Jim; Absolute Quiet; The Devil Doll; Trouble for

Two; Three Wise Guys; We Went to College; Sworn Enemy. 1937 Manproof; Espionage; A Day at the Races; The Good Earth; Rosalie; Badman of Brimstone; Night Must Fall; Saratoga; Song of the City; The Good Old Soak; Live and Learn. 1938 Paradise for Three; The Crowd Roars; Port of Seven Seas; Test Pilot; Too Hot to Handle; Woman Against Woman; Hold That Kiss; Of Human Hearts; The First Hundred Years; Lord Jeff; Yellow Jack; Fast Company; Listen Darling; The Chaser; Rich Man, Poor Girl. 1939 Babes in Arms; Bad Little Angel; Bridal Suite; The Girl Downstairs; On Borrowed Time; Good Enemies; These Glamour Girls; Fast and Loose; Within the Law; Lucky Night; Society Lawyer; Let Freedom Ring w *Valles*; Four Girls in White; Stronger Than Desire; On Borrowed Time; 600 Enemies. 1940 The Captain Is a Lady; Edison the Man w *Steele*; Young Tom Edison w *Steele*; Go West w *Steele*; I Love You Again; Congo Maisie; Strike Up the Band; The Man From Dakota; Sporting Blood; Gold Rush Maisie; Andy Hardy Meets Debutante. 1941 Bad Man w *Valles*; The Penalty; Free and Easy; The Trial of Mary Dugan. 1942 The Magnificent Dope (Fox); The Pied Piper (Fox); Ten Gentlemen From West Point (Fox); Tales of Manhattan w *Irene, Wakeling, Newman*.

Valles (MGM) 1938 Stand up and Fight w *Tree*; A Christmas Carol. 1939 The Adventures of Huckleberry Flynn; Bad Little Angel w *Tree*; Maisie w *Tree*; Balalaika w *Adrian*; Thunder Afloat w *Tree*; The Kid From Texas w *Tree*; Broadway Serenade w *Adrian*; Let Freedom Ring w *Tree*; At the Circus w *Tree*. 1940 The Broadway Melody of 1940 w *Adrian*. 1944 Dragon Seed; Mrs Parkington w *Keyes*; National Velvet w *Dean*; The Picture of Dorian Gray w *Keyes*; Lost in a Harem w *Dean*. 1945 Her Highness and the Bellboy w *Keyes*. 1946 Easy to Wed w *Irene*; The Green Years; The Harvey Girls w *Rose*; Holiday in Mexico w *Irene*; Two Sisters From Boston w *Rose*; The Yearling. 1947 Green Dophin Street w *Plunkett*; This Time for Keeps w *Irene*; Sea of Grass w *Plunkett*. 1948 Easter Parade w *Irene*; Words and Music w *Rose*. 1949 Barkleys of Broadway w *Irene*; Big Jack; The Great Sinner w *Irene*; In the Good Old Summertime w *Irene*; Madame Bovary w *Plunkett*; Take Me Out to the Ballgame w *Rose*; That Forsythe Woman w *Plunkett*; That Midnight Kiss w *Rose*. 1950 Kim. 1951 Adventures of Captain Fabian (Rep). 1960 Spartacus (U) w *Thomas*.

Natalie Visart (Par) 1934 Cleopatra w *Jester, Banton, Shannon Rogers, Vicki*. 1935 The Crusades w *Banton*. 1937 The Plainsman w *Franklin*. 1938 The Buccaneer. 1939 Union Pacific. 1941 Meet Joe Doe (WB). 1942 Reap the Wild Wind. 1943 Lady of Burlesque (UA–Stromberg). 1944 Guest in the House (UA– Stromberg); Story of Dr Wassell. 1945 Young Widow (UA– Stromberg); The Strange Woman (UA–Stromberg).

Sophie Wachner (1922–3 Goldwyn; 1924 MGM; 1925–30 Fox) 1922 The Wallflower. 1923 The Eternal Three; Look Your

Best; Three Wise Fools; Red Lights; Nellie the Beautiful Cloak Model; Six Days; In the Palace of the King; Name in Man; The Day of Faith; Reno; Wild Oranges. 1924 Daring Love (Truart); He Who Gets Slapped; His Hour; Married Flirts; The Snob; Three Weeks; Wife of the Centaur; So This Is Marriage. 1925 The Great Divide. 1928 Red Wine. 1929 Big Time; Fox Movietone Follies of 1929; Happy Days; Hot for Paris; Love Live and Laugh; Married in Hollywood; Dix on Dames; Pleasure Crazed; Romance of the Rio Grande; Seven Faces; A Song of Kentucky; South Sea Rose; Speakeasy; Sunny Side Up; They Had to See Paris; Thru Different Eyes; Words and Music. 1930 Are You There?; The Arizona Kid; The Big Party; Cameo Kirby; City Girl; Common Clay; Crazy That Way; The Dancers; A Devil With Women; Double Cross Roads; Fox Movietone Follies of 1930; The Golden Calf; High Society Blues; Just Imagine w O'Neill; Last of the Duanes; Lightnin'; Lilliom; The Lone Star Ranger; Man Trouble; Not Damaged; Oh, for a Man!; On the Level; On Your Back; The Princess and the Plumber; Renegades; Scotland Yard; So This Is London; Song O' My Heart; Such Men Are Dangerous; Up the River; Wild Company; Women Everywhere. 1936 Little Lord Fauntleroy (UA–Selznick).

Gwen Wakeling (1929–30 Pat; 1931–2 RKO; 1933–4 UA-20th; 1935–42 Fox)
1927 The Girl In the Pullman (DeM); King of Kings (DeM) w Luick. 1928 The Desert Song (WB) w Luick. 1929 Paris Bound; The Racketeer; Red Hot Rhythm; Rich People; This Thing Called Love. 1930 Holiday; Big Money; The Grand Parade; Her Man; Officer O'Brien; Sin Takes a Holiday; Swing High. 1931 Devotion (RKO); The Common Law (RKO). 1932 Carnival Boat (RKO). 1933 Broadway Through a Keyhole (UA–20th); Gallant Lady (UA–20th). 1934 The Affairs of Cellini (UA–20th); Born to Be Bad (UA–20th); Bulldog Drummond Strikes Back (UA–20th); The Count of Monte Cristo (UA–Small); The House of Rothschild (UA–20th); The Last Gentleman (UA–20th); Transatlantic Merry-Go-Round (UA–Small). 1935 King of Burlesque; The Littlest Rebel; The Man Who Broke the Bank at Monte Carlo. 1936 Captain January; The Country Doctor; Dimples; Everybody's Old Man; Girls Dormitory; Half Angel; It Had to Happen; Banjo on My Knee; Pigskin Parade; The Poor Little Rich Girl; The Prisoner of Shark Island; Private Number; Ramona; The Road to Glory; Under Two Flags; White Hunter. 1937 Ali Baba Goes to Town w Herschel; Alexander's Ragtime Band; Danger, Love at Work; Heidi; Love Under Fire; Nancy Steele is Missing; On the Avenue; Seventh Heaven; Wee Willie Winkie; Wife, Doctor and Nurse; Wake Up and Live. 1938 The Baroness and the Butler; Gateway; I'll Give a Million; Just Around the Corner; Kentucky; Kidnapped; Little Miss Broadway; Rebecca of Sunnybrook Farm; Sally, Irene and Mary; Straight, Place and Show; Submarine Patrol; Thanks for Everything; Three Blind Mice. 1939 The Adventures of Sherlock Holmes; Hotel for Women; The Gorilla; The Hound of the Baskervilles; The Little Princess; The Rains Came; The Return of the Cisco Kid; Second Honeymoon; Susannah of the Mounties; Tail Spin. 1940 The Blue Bird;

Brigham Young; Grapes of Wrath; He Married His Wife; Johnny Apollo; Stardust; Young People. 1941 Confirm or Deny; I Wake Up Screaming; Rise and Shine; Swamp Water; Weekend in Havana. 1942 Moontide; My Gal Sal; Remember the Day; Rings on Her Fingers; Roxie Hart; Son of Fury; Tales of Manhattan w Tree, Irene, Newman; This Above All; To the Shores of Tripoli. 1944 Cover Girl (Col) w Banton, King. 1947 Unconquered (Par) w Karinska. 1951 Valentino (Col) w Banton. 1954 The High and the Mighty (WB); Cattle Queen of Montana (Rep). 1955 Blood Alley (WB); Escape to Burma (RKO); Tennessee's Partner (RKO). 1956 Great Day in the Morning (RKO); Johnny Concho (UA). 1966 Frankie and Johnny (UA–Small).

Tony Walton
1964 Mary Poppins (BV) w Thomas. 1966 A Funny Thing Happened on the Way to the Forum (UA). 1968 Petulia (WB); The Sea Gull (WB). 1974 Murder on the Orient Express (Par).

Claire West (1918–24 Par)
1915 Birth of a Nation. 1916 Intolerance. 1919 Male and Female. 1921 The Affairs of Anatol. 1922 Saturday Night. 1923 Adam's Rib; Bella Donna. 1924 The Ten Commandments w Greer; The Goldfish (FN); For Sale (FN); Flirting With Love (FN); The Lady (FN); Sherlock Jr (RGM). 1925 The Golden Bed (Par); The Merry Widow (MGM).

Vera West (U)
1927 The Man Who Laughs w Cox. 1930 King of Jazz. 1932 The Mummy; Back Street. 1933 Ladies Must Love; Only Yesterday; The Secret of the Blue Room. 1934 Cheating Cheaters; Gift of Gab; I Like It That Way; Let's Be Ritzy; One More River; Glamour; Little Man What Now. 1935 Diamond Jim; The Man Who Reclaimed His Head; Remember Last Night; The Good Fairy. 1936 Next Time We Love; Showboat. 1937 One Hundred Men and a Girl. 1938 Letter of Introduction; The Rage of Paris; Sinners in Paradise; Swing That Cheer; That Certain Age; Youth Takes a Fling; Mad About Music. 1939 Destry Rides Again; East Side of Paradise; First Love; For Love or Money; Hero for a Day; The Sun Never Sets; Three Smart Girls Grow Up. 1940 It's a Date; My Little Chickadee; Seven Sinners w Irene; The Mummy's Hand; Private Affairs; The Bank Dick; Ski Patrol; South of Karanja; Spring Parade. 1941 Sing Another Chorus; Back Street w Murial King; It Started With Eve; Keep 'Em Flying; Never Give a Sucker an Even Break; The Black Cat; Badlands of Dakota; Hellzapoppin'; Hold that Ghost; Nice Girl; The Lady From Cheyenne; The Man Who Lost Himself; Model Wife w Royer; Where Did You Get That Girl; The Wolf Man. 1942 Almost Married; Eagle Squadron; Pardon My Sarong; Pittsburgh; The Spoilers; Broadway; Fighting Bill Fargo; The Ghost of Frankenstein; Halfway to Shanghai. Invisible Agent; Moonlight in Havana; Ride 'Em Cowboy; Sin Town; The Great Impersonation. 1943 The Phantom of the Opera; The Strange Death of Adolph Hitler; The Amazing Mrs Holliday; Crazy Horse; Cracked Nuts; Flesh and Fantasy w Head; She's for Me; Hers to Hold w

Adrian; His Butler's Sister w *Adrian*; Hit the Ice; Larceny With Music; Shadow of a Doubt w *Adrian*. 1944 This Is the Life; The Suspect; South of Dixie; Slightly Terrific; The Singing Sheriff; San Diego, I Love You; Phantom Lady; The Pearl of Death; The Merry Monohans; The Mummy's Ghost; Follow the Boys w *Greer*; Weird Woman; Swingtime Johnny; Bowery to Broadway; Christmas Holiday w *Greer, King*; The Climax; Cobra Woman; Dead Man's Eyes; Gypsy Wildcat; Her Primitive Man; In Society; The Invisible Man's Revenge; Ladies Courageous. 1945 Song of the Sarong; Here Come the Co-eds; Frisco Sal; Her Lucky Night; House of Frankenstein; Men in Her Diary; The Naughty Nineties; Patrick the Great; Pillow of Death; Pursuit to Algiers; Salome, Where She Danced; Shady Lady; She Gets Her Man; Strange Confession; Under Western Skies; Sudan; Swing Out Sister. 1946 Black Angel; Danger Woman; I'll Be Yours w *Banton*; The Killers; Magnificent Doll w *Banton*; Pirates of Monterey w *Banton*; She Wrote the Book; Slightly Scandalous; Smooth as Silk; The Spider Woman Strikes Back. 1947 The Egg and I.

Miles White

1946 The Kid From Brooklyn (RKO–Goldwyn) w *Louis*. 1952 The Greatest Show on Earth (Par) w *Head, Jeakins*. 1955 There's No Business Like Show Business (Fox) w *Travilla*. 1956 Around the World in Eighty Days (UA–Todd).

Mary Wills (1949–52 RKO–Goldwyn; 1955–8 Fox)

1949 My Foolish Heart; Roseanna McCoy. 1950 Our Very Own. 1951 I Want You. 1952 Hans Christian Anderson w *Clave, Karinska*. 1955 Good Morning, Miss Dove; The Virgin Queen. 1956 Between Heaven and Hell; Bigger Than Life; Carousel; The Last Wagon; Love Me Tender; Teenage Rebel; The True Story of Jesse James. 1957 Bernardine; A Hatful of Rain; No Down Payment; The Wayward Bus. 1958 The Diary of Anne Frank; A Certain Smile; Sing Boy Sing; Fraulein.

Yvonne Wood (1942–5 Fox; 1946–50 U)

1942 Orchestra Wives. 1943 The Gang's All Here. 1944 The Big Noise Greenwich Village; Something For the Boys; Sweet and Lowdown; Tampico. 1945 Circumstantial Evidence; Doll Face; Molly and Me; Thunderhead, Son of Flicka; A Bell for Adano. 1946 Swell Guy. 1947 Ride the Pink Horse; Slave Girl; Song of Scheherezade; The Web. 1948 An Act of Murder; Another Part of the Forest; Black Bart; A Double Life w *Banton*; Mexican Hayride; River Lady; Tap Roots. 1949 Baghdad; Criss Cross; The Gal Who Took the West; Illegal Entry. 1950 Comanche Territory; Double Crossbones; Frenchie; Shakedown; Winchester '73. 1952 Just for You (Par) w *Head*; Lady in the Iron Mask (Fox); San Francisco Story (WB); Casanova's Big Night (Par). 1953 Fort Algiers (UA); Raiders of the Seven Seas (UA); Red Garters (Par) w *Head*. 1956 The Conqueror (RKO) w *Woulfe*; The Court Jester (Par) w *Head*. 1958 The Big Country (UA) w *Santiago*; Man of the West (UA–Mirisch). 1960 Lil' Abner (Par); Botany Bay (Par). 1961 One-Eyed Jacks (Par). 1966 Duel at Diablo (UA). 1968 Firecreek (WB); Guns for San

Sebastian (MGM). 1970 The Cheyenne Social Club (Nat Gen); Dirty Dingus Magee (MGM). 1971 The Outfit (MGM). 1973 Judge Roy Bean (Nat Gen) w *Head*.

Michael Woulfe (RKO)

1945 Blood on the Sun (UA–Cagney). 1946 The Stranger (RKO–International); The Searching Wind (Par) w *Dorothy O'Hara*; Love From a Stranger (EL); Abie's Irish Rose (UA–Crosby). 1947 Singapore (U); Tycoon w *Franklin*; Mr Ace (UA); The Locket. 1949 A Dangerous Profession. 1950 The Woman on Pier 13; Roadblock; Gambling House; Where Danger Lives; Gun Notches; Born to Be Bad w *Hattie Carnegie*; Flying Leathernecks; The White Tower; Terror; The Secret Fury; Bail Bond Story; The Company She Keeps. 1951 A Girl in Every Port; My Forbidden Past; The Racket; Sealed Cargo; Best of the Badmen; The Thing; Gaunt Woman; Arizona Ambush; Armed Car Robbery. 1952 Macao; One Minute to Zero; The Half Breed; The Lusty Men; Angel Face; Beware, My Lovely; Outpost in Malaya (UA); Blackbeard the Pirate; Marry Me Again; Two Tickets to Broadway; Son of Sinbad. 1953 She Couldn't Say No; Devil's Canyon; Clash by Night; Split Second; Affair With a Stranger; Second Chance. 1954 Susan Slept Here; The French Line w *Greer*; Dangerous Mission; The Americano; This Is My Love. 1955 Glory; Texas Lady; Bengazi; Underwater. 1956 The Conqueror w *Wood*. 1957 Jet Pilot (RKO). 1971 Happy Birthday Wanda June (Col).

Paul Zastupnevich (Fox)

1959 The Big Circus (AA). 1960 The Lost World. 1961 Voyage to the Bottom of the Sea. 1962 Five Weeks in a Balloon. 1974 The Towering Inferno.

Index